D1137461

mustsees
ROME

The dome of St Peter's Basilica   E. Zane/MICHELIN

MICHELIN

General Manager   Cynthia Clayton Ochterbeck

mustsees Rome

Editorial Manager	Jonathan P. Gilbert
Editorial	JMS Books, Jo Murray
Contributing Writers	Charlotte Hurdman, Andrew Kirk, Linda Lee, Jackie Strachan
Production Manager	Natasha G. George
Cartography	Stephane Anton, John Dear, Thierry Lemasson
Photo Editor	Yoshimi Kanazawa
Photo Researcher	Emma O'Neill
Layout	Chris Bell, cbdesign, Satzomatic
Cover & Interior Design	Chris Bell, cbdesign

Contact Us	Michelin Maps and Guides
	One Parkway South
	Greenville, SC 29615
	USA
	www.michelintravel.com
	Michelin Maps and Guides
	Hannay House
	39 Clarendon Road
	Watford, Herts WD17 1JA
	UK
	☏ (01923) 205 240
	www.ViaMichelin.com
	travelpubsales@uk.michelin.com

Special Sales	For information regarding bulk sales, customized editions and premium sales, please contact our Customer Service Departments:	
	USA	1-800-432-6277
	UK	(01923) 205 240
	Canada	1-800-361-8236

Michelin Apa Publications Ltd
A joint venture between Michelin and Langenscheidt

58 Borough High Street, London SE1 1XF, United Kingdom

No part of this publication may be reproduced in any form
without the prior permission of the publisher.

© 2010 Michelin Apa Publications Ltd
ISBN 978-1-907099-03-8
Printed: August 2010
Printed and bound: Himmer, Germany

Note to the reader:
While every effort is made to ensure that all information printed in this guide is correct and
up-to-date, Michelin Apa Publications Ltd. accepts no liability for any direct, indirect or
consequential losses howsoever caused so far as such can be excluded by law. Admission
prices listed for sights in this guide are for a single adult, unless otherwise specified.

Welcome to Rome

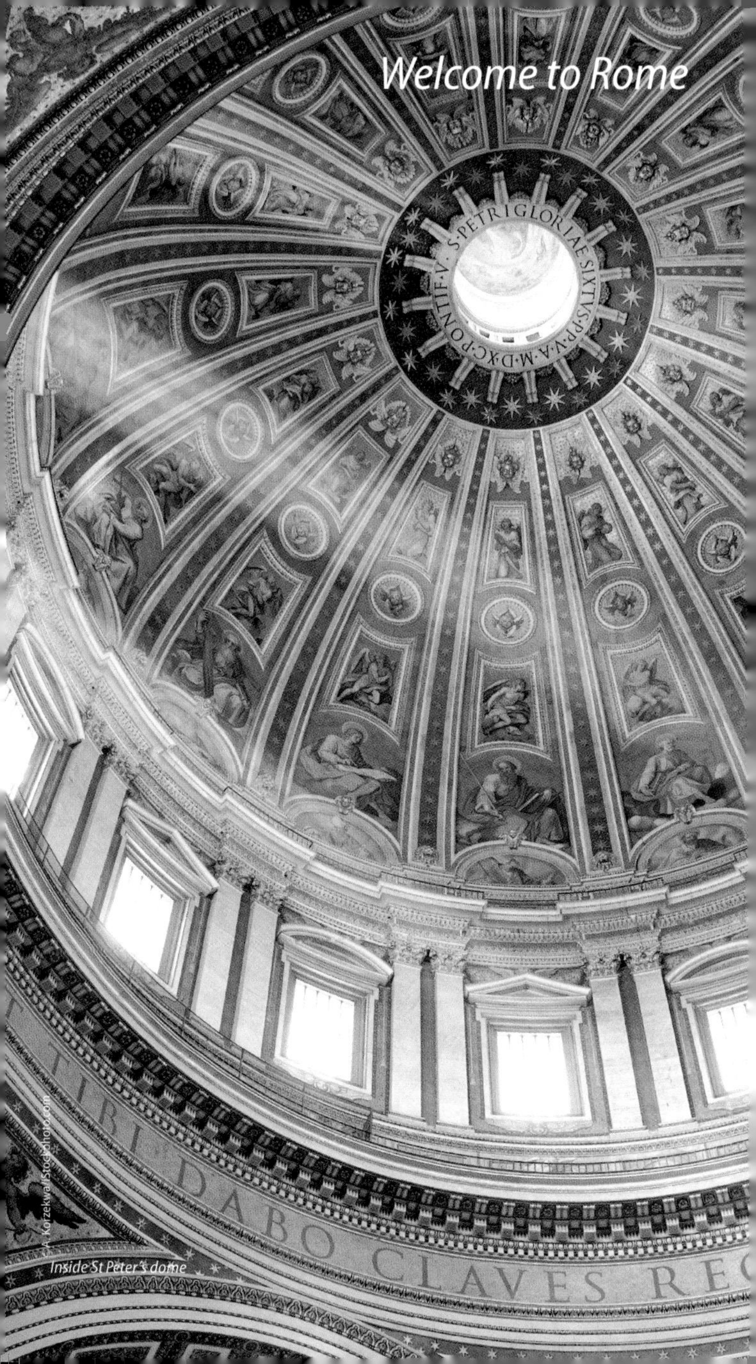

Inside St Peter's dome

p22

©Britta Jaschinski/APA Publications

Introduction

p32

D. Chapuis/MICHELIN

p52

G. Bludzin/MICHELIN

M. Gáspár/MICHELIN

p26

TABLE OF CONTENTS

★★★ ATTRACTIONS

Unmissable historic and cultural sights

Piazza di Spagna p 54

S. Fredaigue/MICHELIN

Angel Musician, by Melozzo da Forli, Vatican Museum p 26

B. Pérousse/MICHELIN

Roman Forum, Colonna di Foca p 32

D. Chapuis/MICHELIN

St Peter's Basilica p 24

©Antoine Beyeler/iStockphoto.com

MUST KNOW

Pantheon, Piazza della Rotonda p 92

Piazza Navona p 62

Villa Borghese p 102

G. Bludzin/MICHELIN

M.Marca/MICHELIN

G. Bludzin/MICHELIN

Colosseum p 46

Hadrian's Villa, Tivoli p 106

Piazza del Campidoglio p 30

Trevi Fountain p 100

MUST KNOW

 # ACTIVITIES

Unmissable activities and entertainment

©Simone Cecchetti, 2010/courtesy Zaha Hadid Architects

MAXXI (National Museum of XXI Century Arts) p 91

©Il Gelato di S. Crispino

Il Gelato di S.Crispino p 119

©Britta Jaschinski/APA Publications

Via dei Condotti p 55

G. Bludzin/MICHELIN

Foro Italico p 120

STAR ATTRACTIONS

Unmissable historic, cultural, and natural sights

For more than 75 years people have used Michelin stars to take the guesswork out of travel. Our star-rating system helps you make the best decision on where to go, what to do, and what to see.

★★★	Unmissable
★★	Worth a trip
★	Worth a detour
No star	recommended

MUST KNOW

ACTIVITIES

**Unmissable
entertainment,
activities, and
restaurants.**

Outings

Admire the views from
   the Gianicolo *p104*
Cycle along Via Appia
   Antica *p117*
Enjoy the Estate
   Romana Festival *p133*
Jazz concerts at Villa
   Celimontana *p105*
See contemporary art
   at MAXXI *p91*

Kids

Bioparco in the
   Villa Borghese
   Gardens *p102*
Explore Museo
   Explora! *p117*
Put your hand in the
   della Bocca della
   Verità *p70*

Sports

See a soccer match *p120*
Swim in the Piscina
   delle Rose *p118*
Visit the Foro
   Italico *p120*

Shopping

Il Tridente *p77*
Market in the Piazza
   Campo dei Fiori *p124*
Via dei Condotti *p55*

Food/Drink

Caffé Greco *p55*
Dine on Via Veneto *p78*
Try an ice cream *p119*

Nightlife

Alexanderplatz *p129*
Centri Sociali *p132*
Via di Monte
   Testaccio *p131*

STAR ATTRACTIONS

CALENDAR OF EVENTS

You can get more details of events and festivals from the Vatican Information Office (Ufficio Informazioni Pellegrini e Turisti) and from local tourist offices (APT).

January

Festival of the Befana
The last of the Twelve Days of Christmas; market stalls in Piazza Navona overflow with toys and sweets and Befana, the good witch, brings presents to children *(Jan 6)*

Feast of St Agnes
In the Church of Sant'Agnese Fuori le Mura, two lambs are blessed and their wool is made into *palliums* to be presented to each new archbishop by the pope *(Jan 21)*

February

Remembrance of Giordano Bruno
Executed by the Inquisition, freethinker Bruno is honored with music and masked dancers at his statue in Rome's Campo dei Fiori *(Feb 17)*

March

EuroChocolate Festival
Nine days of lectures, tastings, films, and gorging on chocolate *(www.eurochocolate.roma.it. Early Mar)*

International Women's Day
Mothers, sisters, and grandmothers are celebrated and presented with yellow mimosa blossoms *(Mar 8)*

Blessing of automobiles
Drivers gather near the Church of Santa Francesca Romana, patron saint of drivers *(Mar 9)*

Feast of St Joseph
In the Trionfale district stalls mark the saint's day by selling *bignè*, a kind of doughnut, and *frittelle*, made from choux pastry *(Mar 19)*

Beginning of spring
Explore Italy's private gardens, monasteries, villas, and castles for free *(weekend closest to Mar 21)*

Rome Marathon
Thousands of runners pound past the city's ruins *(www.maratoneta.it. Third Sat)*

April

Good Friday
Stations of the Cross marked by night between the Colosseum and the Palatine Hill

Easter Day
At noon in St Peter's Square the pope gives his *Urbi et Orbi* blessing

Anniversary of the founding of Rome
Solemn ceremony on the Capitoline Hill to commemorate the birth of the city in 753 BC *(Apr 21)*

Liberation Day
Marking the end of the German occupation in 1945 *(Apr 25)*

May

May Day
A public holiday marked with parades and speeches in honor of the nation's workers *(May 1)*

Antique Fair in Via dei Coronari
Stalls crammed with furniture and antiques line this historic street *(throughout the month)*

Roseto di Roma

Roses in bloom in the municipal rose gardens in Via di Valle Murcia *(throughout the month)*

June

Feast of St John

Festival in the district bearing the saint's name, with games and events *(Jun 23–24)*

Feast of St Peter and St Paul

Service in St Peter's Basilica on the most solemn of the religious festivals in Rome *(Jun 29)*

July

Tevere-Expo

A large fair selling handicrafts and local foodstuffs on the banks of the Tiber, with open-air concerts and dancing

Festa de'Noantri

A week of singing, dancing and feasting in Trastevere to celebrate the unique character of this colorful district *(Jul 15–30)*

Estate Romana

Held at venues all around the city, this open-air festival features concerts and cabaret shows, and film screenings *(Jul and Aug)*

Villa Celimontana Jazz Festival

Rome's premier jazz festival brings together stars from around the world *(Jul and Aug)*

August

Flower petals in Santa Maria Maggiore

Flower petals cascade down onto the congregation to commemorate the miraculous fall of snow that led to the construction of the church *(Aug 5)*

Feast of the Assumption

Public holiday across the whole of Italy *(Aug 15)*

September

European Heritage Day

Private gardens and palaces open their doors *(4th Sun)*

October

Crafts and exhibitions in Via Orso

Throughout the month

Great Autumn Antique Market

Held at the Autodromo di Vallelunga, the largest antiques market in the region, selling everything from memorabilia and curios to vintage cars and antique furniture

November

All Saint's Day

Costumed children race through the squares, flinging confetti and shaving cream *(Nov 1)*

December

Christmas Fair in Piazza Navona

A month-long fair selling candies, festive ornaments, and toys, with a carrousel for children and street entertainers, illuminated prettily at night

Feast of the Immaculate Conception

Celebration in Piazza di Spagna in the presence of the pope *(Dec 8)*

Christmas

Annual exhibition in Via Giulia of over 50 nativity scenes, with beautiful cribs in the nearby churches

Christmas Eve

Midnight mass is celebrated with particular solemnity in the churches of Santa Maria Maggiore and Santa Maria d'Aracoeli

PRACTICAL INFORMATION

WHEN TO GO

Rome's mild Mediterranean climate makes it bright and crisp in winter, hot in summer. April, May, September, and October have sunny skies and mild temperatures and these months attract the most visitors (especially over Easter). The heat of August is oppressive so the Romans head for the hills and many of the city's shops and restaurants are closed. The wettest month is November with heavy downpours leading to falling temperatures. In winter, the air is fresh but you may not even need a coat in December, though in February, snow flurries are possible before the mild weather returns in March.

KNOW BEFORE YOU GO

A little homework before you depart will help you get the most out of your trip.

Useful websites

www.060608.it – Rome tourism's new website lists sights, events and exhibitions, and accommodation.
www.turismoroma.it – Rome's official tourist website lists regularly updated addresses, transport details, events, and children's activities.
www.wantedinrome.com – A site for locals but useful for tourists too containing news, cultural listings, and advertisements for accommodation. Other websites worth a look include:
www.capitolium.org
www.cinecittastudios.it
www.centroguideroma.net
www.touringclub.it

Tourist information

Rome's main tourist information office is: **APT (Azienda Promozionale Turistica di Roma)** – Via Parigi 5–11. 06 48 89 91. www.turismoroma.it. A new APT service offers a comprehensive source of information for visitors in English. Call 06 06 08 or visit www.060608.it.

Green tourist information points—called PIT *(Punti Informativi Turistici)*—can be found at places such as Fiumicino airport, Termini railway station, Castel Sant'Angelo, Piazza delle Cinque Lune (Piazza Navona), Via Nazionale (opposite the Palazzo delle Esposizioni), Santa Maria Maggiore, Trastevere (Piazza Sidney Sonnino).

International visitors

Australian Embassy:
06 85 27 21
www.italy.embassy.gov.au/rome/home.html
Canadian Embassy:
06 85 444 2911
www.canada.it
Irish Embassy:
06 69 79 121
www.embassyofireland.it
New Zealand Embassy:
06 853 7501
www.nzembassy.com/italy
South African Embassy:
06 852 541
www.sudafrica.it
UK Embassy:
06 42 20 00 01
www.ukinitaly.fco.gov.uk
USA Embassy:
06 46 74 1
rome.usembassy.gov

Entry requirements

Passports – EU nationals entering Italy need only a national identity card. Nationals of other countries must be in possession of a valid national passport. In case of loss or theft, report to the embassy or consulate and the local police.

Visas – Entry visas are required by Australian, New Zealand, Canadian, and US citizens if their stay exceeds 3 months. Apply to the Italian Consulate (visa issued same day; delay if submitted by mail). US citizens may find it useful to search Tips for Traveling Abroad on the Department of State travel advice website travel.state.gov.

Customs regulations

The US Customs and Border Protection's publication *Know Before You Go* for US citizens can be downloaded from www.cbp. gov. Americans can bring home, tax-free, up to US$800 worth of goods; Canadians up to CND$300; Australians up to AUS$400 and New Zealanders up to NZ$700. For EU citizens there are no limits to purchasing goods for personal use, but there are recommended allowances for alcoholic beverages and tobacco.

GETTING THERE
By Air

Two airports serve Rome: Leonardo da Vinci (Fiumicino) Airport is Rome's international airport, while Ciampino is smaller and used mainly for domestic and European charter flights. For details on how to get to and from the airports and central Rome see the Aeroporti di Roma website: www.adr.it.

Leonardo da Vinci (Fiumicino) Airport – 06 65 95. www.adr.it. 16mi/26km southwest of Rome on the A91.

Ciampino Airport – 06 65 951. www.adr.it. 10mi/15km southeast of Rome on the SS7.

By Train

The main stations in Rome are **Termini** *(Piazza dei Cinquecento)* and **Tiburtina** *(Piazza della Stazione Tiburtina)*. Both stations are well connected to Rome's public transport system via the metro and numerous buses, which leave from outside the station. The nationally owned rail company is Ferrovie dello Stato, which owns **Trenitalia**. For information on times and ticket prices see the websites www.ferroviedellostato.it and www.trenitalia.com or call 89 20 21 *(information in Italian 24hr)*— 00 39 06 68 475 475 if calling from outside Italy. For information for disabled travelers call 199 30 30 60. **Italia Rail** is a website dedicated to train travel in Italy and is run by official agents for Trenitalia, www. italiarail.com.

You can purchase tickets from automated machines at the rail station, which have menus in English. Tickets are good for 2 months, but must be stamped before boarding or you may get a fine. Orange validation machines are at the end of platforms. Several towns near Rome—such as Viterbo, Pantano, and Ostia— are accessible by train: the Rome– Viterbo line leaves from Piazzale Flaminio Station; Rome–Pantano from Roma Laziali Station; the Rome–Lido line leaves from Porta San Paolo Station and makes three stops before Ostia Lido, one of which is the ruins at Ostia Antica.

By Bus

There is no central bus station in Rome, so buses depart and terminate in front of Tiburtina station. **Eurolines** *(06 6662 3156; www. eurolines.com)* runs international buses with connections to cities throughout Europe. Journeys are long and slow, but fares are cheap.

By Car

On the outer edge of the city is the Grande Raccordo Anulare (GRA), a multilane ring road from which all the motorways and main roads *(strada statale)* radiate. The Tangenziale Est links the Stadio Olimpico to Piazza San Giovanni in Laterano via such eastern quarters as Nomentano, Tiburtino, and Prenestino. **Car rental agencies** require a credit card, passport, license, and a driver over 21 or 23. Non-EU citizens may wish to carry an international driving license, obtainable in the US from the American Automobile Association (www.aaa.com). Other documents required include the vehicle's current logbook and a certificate of motor insurance. Be sure to check the rental insurance terms carefully—some policies will not cover an accident that does not include a third party e.g. a collision with a wall.

Cars are not permitted to enter the historic center of Rome without an official pass, which you can purchase from most car rental companies *(see p 18)*. The limited traffic area is marked with the letters ZTL in black on a yellow background. If you pass this sign your registration number will be caught on camera and notice of a fine—or fines if you cross more than one ZTL zone—could be sent to your home address. Regulations such as drinking and driving (limited to 0.5g/l) and driving without a license are usually enforced by on-the-spot fines (typically €150–250). Failure to pay a fine at the time may result in the confiscation of your vehicle.

The American Automobile Association has a reciprocal agreement with the **Automobile Club d'Italia** *(ACI Via Marsala 8, 00185 Rome; call 06 49 1115/803 116 (helpline); www.aci.it)* for breakdown assistance and general information. For further information on driving in Italy see www. theaa.com/motoring_advice/ touring_tips/AA-italy-san-marino. pdf. For information on driving on motorways *(autostrade)*, which are subject to a toll, see www. autostrade.it.

GETTING AROUND

The best way to explore Rome is by foot and on public transport—Rome's streets are narrow and the historic center is increasingly pedestrianized. Traffic in the city is heavy and parking places are difficult to find.

By Public Transport

Rome has an integrated public transport system organized by **ATAC** *(Azienda Tramvie e Autobus del Comune di Roma)*. Metrebus tickets *(biglietti)* work on all metro lines, buses, and trams in the urban area (but not on services to the airports). Tickets can be bought from *tabacchi* (tobacconists—look for the "T" signs outside), newsstands, at metro stations, and end-of-line bus stops. A single ticket costs €1 and is valid for 75min from the moment it is first stamped. Within those 75min you are entitled to use any combination of buses, trams, and one metro journey. You will need to stamp your ticket in the yellow machines when getting on the bus or tram, and/or put it through the turnstile when entering the metro.

A 1-day pass costs €4 and lasts from the moment you stamp it until midnight of the same day. A 3-day pass costs €11 and lasts from the moment you stamp it until midnight of the third day. A 7-day pass costs €16 and lasts from the moment you stamp it until midnight of the seventh day. A monthly pass is also available for €30.

City route plans are on sale in bookshops and kiosks; the plan *Rete dei Trasporti Urbani di Roma*, published by ATAC, is sold at the Termini tourist information point in Piazza dei Cinquecento.

By Bus

Buses operate from 5.30am until midnight. *Fermata* (bus stop) signs list the routes of the buses that stop there. A request stop is called *fermata richiesta*. The entrance door *(salita)* is at the back of the bus and the exit *(uscita)* in the middle. The following routes are among the most useful for tourists: **64** and **40** from Termini station to the Vatican, stopping at Via Nazionale, Piazza Venezia, near the Gesù Church, Largo Argentina, and Corso Vittorio Emanuele II. However, beware of pickpockets, notably at rush hour.

116 and **117** run through the historic center using electric minibuses.

714 from Termini to Santa Maria Maggiore, San Giovanni in Laterano, Baths of Caracalla, and EUR.

H from Termini, along Via Nazionale, Piazza Venezia, Largo Argentina, Ponte Garibaldi, and Trastevere.

Hop-on, hop-off buses – Many companies operate open-air tour buses in town, but the **110** is run by the City transport authority. A ticket is valid for 24hr, full price €20; reductions for Roma Pass holders, and children aged 6–12 €15. Buses depart every 20min from Piazza dei Cinquecento *(in front of Termini station)*, 8.30am–8.30pm. The total tour makes 11 stops and takes 2hr with a commentary in English. They also operate **Archeobus**, a service that departs every 30min from Piazza dei Cinquecento 8.30am–4.30pm bound for the beautiful and historic Via Appia Antica park. It makes 14 stops at historic sites and monuments. Tickets are €15 *(children age 6–12 €10)*. A joint ticket for the 110 Open bus and the Archeobus can be purchased for €24 *(valid for 2 days)*. For more information call 06 689 2670, or 800 281 281, www.trambusopen.com.

By Tram

Trams run 5am–9pm. There are 6 lines; the most useful to tourists is line 8, which connects Largo Argentina with Trastevere station and up to Monteverde.

By Metro

Rome's rich archeological history means that the city's subway *(la Metropolitana)* is a simple two-line system that skirts around the historic center, intersecting at Termini railway station. The metro is efficient and safe, but stay on guard for pickpockets and groping in crowds. Trains operate 5.30am–11.30pm *(Sat 12.30am)*, the section Termini–Rebibbia runs until 9pm weekdays and 11pm weekends and holidays.

Line A runs from Battistini to Via Anagnina. The most useful stops include Cipro (the Vatican), Ottaviano (for St Peter's), Spagna (Spanish Steps and Villa Borghese), Barberini (Trevi Fountain).

Line B runs from Rebibbia to Laurentina. Useful stops include Cavour (Piazza Cavour), Colosseo (Colosseum, Forum, Palatine Hill), Circo Massimo (Circus Maximus and the Baths of Caracalla), and Piramide (Mausoleum of Cestius).

By Taxi
To call a taxi dial: 06 35 70; 06 49 94; 06 88 177; 06 41 57; 06 55 51; or 06 66 45.

The basic fixed starting charge is €2.80, rising €0.92/km. Extra charges apply for luggage, night service, Sun and holidays. Flat rates exist for each airport—Fiumicino €40 and Ciampino €30—but expect fare melodrama nonetheless. For a detailed breakdown of taxi tariffs log on to www.comune.roma.it.

By Car
Driving in Rome is not advised as access to the city center is very difficult and parking severely restricted; many streets are reserved for pedestrians, taxis, buses, and local residents. The historic center is delineated as blue zone *(fascia blu)*, from which private cars are excluded Mon–Fri 6.30am–6pm and Sat 2–6pm.

If you must drive into Rome, then parking meters charge €1.03 per hr, except on weekends and evenings. Avoid streets marked *"Sosta Vietata"* (no parking) no matter how many cars cluster there—illegally parked vehicles may be towed (call the city traffic police on 06 67 691). Hotel car parks are the best option, but large parking lots include the Villa Borghese (Piazza Brasile), Parcheggio Ludovisi (Via Ludovisi); Parking Termini (near the train station) and Terminal Gianicolo (Via Gregorio VII). Other ACI car parks are scattered at random around town.

By Bike and Scooter
Both are a good way to get around the lanes and piazzas of the historic center where motorized traffic is either banned or restricted, providing you exercise extreme caution—Rome's traffic is notorious. Scooters *(motorini)* can enter the historic center and park free in blue-line areas.

Bicycles can be rented in the city center, e.g. from Piazza di Spagna, near the entrance to the metro; or from the Villa Borghese. Prices start at about €3–4 an hour or €8–13 all day. Brave souls can rent scooters (and bikes as well) from Romarent *(Vicolo dei Bovari 7a, near the Piazza Navona; 06 689 6555; http://web.tiscali.it/romarent)*; EcoMoveRent *(Via Varese 48/50; 06 44 704 518; www.ecomoverent.com)*; and Bici&Baci *(Via del Viminale 5; 06 482 8443)*. Scooter rental costs from about €35 a day.

By Boat
For an unusual view of the city, take a boat trip on the River Tiber. *Batelli di Roma* has hop-on hop-off

cruises *(1hr 10min)* between Apr and Oct *(winter schedules are reduced)*, between Tiberina Island and Cavour Bridge. The boat starts from Ponte Sant'Angelo *(first departure 10am)* and costs €15 *(valid 24hr)*. For information call 06 977 45 498, or visit www.battellidiroma.it.

BASIC INFORMATION
Accessibility

Disabled travelers – Rome isn't fully accessible to disabled travelers; many of its buildings are hundreds of years old and preservation laws prevent alteration to accommodate wheelchairs. However, most major museums have disabled facilities and several metro stops (but not Colosseo) are wheelchair accessible. Many of the city buses now have lower platforms and so are suitable for wheelchair users. Laws have compelled rail stations, airports, hotels, and most restaurants to follow a stricter set of regulations about wheelchair accessibility to restrooms, ticket counters etc. Rome's exceptional effort is the walkway between Piazza Navona and the Trevi Fountain. Not only does smooth brick designate a pedestrian-friendly path, but also Braille plaques explain the landmarks en-route.

Useful contacts include the Roman disability organization CO.IN *(06 712 9011 Mon–Fri 9am–6pm; www.coninsociale.it)*. English-speakers staff the *Roma per Tutti* advice line *(06 571 77094; www.romapertutti.it; open Mon–Fri 9am–5pm)*. The toll free number is only good within Italy *(800 271 027; open Mon–Fri 9am–5pm, Sat 9am–1pm)*.

Accommodation
For a list of suggested accommodation *see Must Stay*.

Communications
Most payphones in Italy now accept only **pre-paid phone-cards** *(schede telefonica)*, which you can buy at newsstands and tobacconists—break off the corner before use. There are international phone booths in major rail stations and a range of pre-paid international phone cards *(carta telefonica internazionale)*, but the cheapest way to call home is with an international plan tied to your home phone account.

Cell phones in Italy use the European standard GSM networks. US and Canadian visitors will need cell phones that are GSM 900 or 1800 to work in Rome. Frequency compatibility problems can be avoided if your phone is a multi-band (tri-band or, especially, quad-band) cell phone.

Area codes – To make a call you must dial the area code (06 for Rome), even when making a local call.

For international calls from Italy dial the long distance code 00, plus the country code (1 for the USA and Canada, 61 for Australia, 64 for New Zealand, 44 for the UK), then the area code and number. If calling from outside Italy, the international code for the country is +39. Therefore for Rome dial +39 (0)6 xx xx…

Rome has firmly embraced the **internet** and there is free, city-subsidized wireless connection throughout much of the central area and main parks. For information and wireless hot spots log on to www.romawireless.com.

PRACTICAL INFORMATION

Discounts

EU citizens aged under 18 and over 65 years old can enter Rome's museums and archeological sites for free, and students, youth under age 25, teachers, and groups are entitled to discounts. Tourist passes are also available, two of the most popular being: the **Archeologia card** €23.50, valid for 7 days, and covering the Colosseum, Palatine, monuments along the Via Appia, and the national museums *(see www.pierreci.it for more information)*; and the **Roma Pass** €25, valid for 3 days, offering free access to the first two sites or museums in the scheme, reduced entrance on others, and free public transport *(see www.romapass.it for more information)*.

There are discounts on train travel for families and groups, children aged 4–12 travel at half-price of the discounted fare, and children under 4 travel free. The **Carta Verde** *(€40, valid for a year)* gives young people a 10% discount on all trains within Italy, and up to 25% when traveling around Europe. For travelers over 60 years of age *(free for 75 years and over)*, the **Carta d'Argento** *(€30, valid for a year)* offers a 15% discount on the Italian section of all routes and 25% off international connections. See www.trenitalia.com for more information.

Electricity

The voltage is 220V, 50 cycles per second, with a two-pin plug. Pack an adaptor for hairdryers, shavers, computers, etc. North American visitors may need a transformer for appliances beyond a laptop. Seek out an electrical *(elettricità)* or hardware *(ferramenta)* store.

Emergency: **General 113**, *Carabinieri* (police) **112**, Ambulance/medical emergencies **118**, Fire department **115**, European SOS **112**

Directory enquiries: **12**

International operator: **170**

Toll-free numbers begin with **147** or **800**

Health

Check your personal insurance to see if it covers you abroad. Usually you must pay any hospital charges up front and apply for reimbursement when you get home. Citizens of the EU are entitled to reduced cost or free medical treatment when visiting Italy and visitors should obtain a European Health Insurance Card (EHIC) before leaving home. Separate travel and medical insurance is recommended. Italian drugstores/pharmacies *(farmacie)* are usually knowledgeable in helping with minor ailments. At night and on Sun, a sign is posted at each drugstore listing those that are open 24hr, which include those at Piazza Barberini 49, Via Arnula 73, and outside Termini station where Via Cavour meets Piazza dei Cinquecento.

Italian water is safe to drink everywhere except on trains and any source signposted *aqua non potabile*.

Money and Currency exchange

The unit of currency is the euro, which is issued in €5, €10, €20, €50, €100, €200, and €500 notes, and in 1, 2, 5, 10, 20, and 50 cent, and €1 and €2 coins. Payment by debit or credit card is widespread in shops, hotels, and restaurants (although some smaller restaurants may not accept plastic—check before ordering) and in gas stations. Money may also be withdrawn from a bank or from ATMs (bancomat), but credit cards may incur interest pending repayment. Currency cards have largely replaced travelers' checks and are widely accepted.

Money can be changed in post offices (except travelers' checks), banks, money-changing bureau (cambio), and at rail stations and airports. Take your passport as ID and look around for the best rates and lowest commission charges. Bureaus de change are useful in that they may be open outside normal banking hours, but may not offer a very good rate.

Business hours

Most businesses, churches, and some museums open at 8 or 9am, shut for lunch (riposo) from 12.30 or 1pm until 3 or 4pm, and close around 6 or 8pm. Many shops now are open orario continuato (open all day) and a few open on Sun as well. Supermarkets often stay open until 10pm. Museums are closed Mon; on other days ticket offices usually shut 30min–1hr before closing time. Ancient monuments, archeological sites, and public parks close about 1hr before dusk, according to the time of year. Most small businesses, shops, and restaurants are closed the first 2 or 3 weeks of Aug.

Banks are usually open Mon–Fri 8.30am–1.30pm and 2.30–4pm. Some branches open in the city center on Sat morning, but most are closed on Sat, Sun, and public holidays.

Post Offices

Post offices (ufficio postale) are open 8.30am–1.50pm (Sat 1pm). Some central branches open weekday afternoons until 6.30pm. The main post office is at Piazza San Silvestro 19, 00187 Roma. It is open day and night.

Public Holidays

A working day is un giorno feriale; giorni festivi include Sat, Sun, and the following public holidays: Epiphany (Jan 6), Easter Sun and Mon, St Mark's Day and Liberation in 1945 (Apr 25), Labor Day (May 1), the Feast of St Peter and St Paul (Jun 29), Assumption and Ferragosto (Aug 15), All Saints' Day (Nov 1), Immaculate Conception (Dec 8), Christmas Day (Dec 25), St Stephen's Day (Dec 26). Rome celebrates the Birth of Rome (Apr 21) as well.

Smoking

Smoking is banned in all public places such as offices, universities, and rail stations and including restaurants, cafés, and clubs etc.

Taxes and Tipping

A sales tax Imposta sul Valore Aggiunto (IVA) mostly lurks unseen, part and parcel of the bill. Visitors from non-EU countries can claim back the IVA on merchandise over €155 in a single shop—ask the store to help you fill out the forms. Italians tip about 5% in a pizzeria or humble trattoria, or just round up to the nearest euro. The rate should rise in more up-market places, but never top 10%. €0.50 tips are appropriate for bar service. Taxi drivers expect around €0.75, as do cloakroom attendants; porters €0.50–€1 per bag.

WELCOME TO ROME

Rome, the eternal city set on seven hills to which all roads lead, one of the most important sites of antiquity, the center of a major world religion, an unparalleled repository of artistic treasures, a place of history, culture, and romance. No other city in the world can compare. No wonder the Romans are still happy to refer to their city as *caput mundi*, the head of the world.

As one of Europe's most popular tourist spots since the days of the Grand Tour, Rome is used to welcoming visitors and pilgrims. Its tourist infrastructure is good, and its oldest museums have been smartened up over the past few years. It's a good idea to follow the local schedule—mornings and late afternoons are the times for activity, with many shops and trattorias closing for an afternoon nap. And if you have inhibitions be prepared to lose them. Romans are abundantly confident and outgoing, and you will hear passionate, animated conversations carried on at top volume everywhere you go. So make the most of your contacts with these warm, welcoming, and sociable people who will happily pass the

time of day, laugh, flirt, and try to follow your faltering attempts at Italian with good humor.

The main focus of any trip to Rome is the historic center, which is traversed by the River Tiber and bounded by the ancient Aurelian Walls. Rome is a whole series of historic eras stacked on top of each other. In this relatively small area are some of the most significant landmarks of antiquity, such as the Colosseum, the Forum, the Imperial Fora, and the Palatine Hill and triumphal arches, temples, and victory columns can be found in almost every neighborhood. Add to this the medieval buildings and churches, the Renaissance palaces and basilicas, the beautiful squares and gardens, and you quickly get the sense of being in

Ice cream shop near Pantheon

INTRODUCTION

an open-air museum. But Rome is far from being weighed down by its history, and the city is noisy, vibrant, and full of life.

For more than 2,000 years, Rome and religion have been synonymous. St Peter's Basilica is the crown jewel in Rome's unmistakable skyline and the centerpiece of the Vatican City, the papal-controlled city-state. As well as being a place of pilgrimage, the Vatican's artistic heritage—from Bernini's colonnade framing St Peter's Square to Michelangelo's frescoes in the Sistine Chapel and the priceless works in the Vatican Museums—make it magnet for visitors of all faiths and none. Rome is thronged with churches of every size and from every era, and if you were so inclined you could spend your entire trip visiting them, though since there are over 900 you would be unlikely to get around them all.

Next to history and religion, food is central to the experience of Rome. Like the city itself, the flavors of Roman cooking are rich and robust, heavy on sauces, meat, and hearty bean stews. Parma ham *(saltimbocca)*, fried sweetbreads, and milk-fed lamb *(abbacchio)* are local specialties, while sea bass *(spigola)* and fried cod *(baccala)* are popular fish alternatives, accompanied by the wines of the surrounding Castelli Romani region. And whether upmarket restaurant or side-street trattoria, the food will inevitably be sourced locally, and served with relaxed respect. For food on the run, the holy trinity of the Italian diet—wafer light pizza, strong coffee, and delicious ice cream—can be found on every corner.

Ostia Antica

©Britta Jaschinski/APA Publications

You can go shopping in the Tridente or Via dei Conditti, or visit the colorful market in the Piazza Campo dei Fiori, or examine the craft shops of Via Margutta. You can take a boat out on the lake in the Borghese Gardens, or if you are feeling very athletic you could cycle out into the countryside along Via Appia Antica. Or you could just find a café, order a ristretto, and enjoy the passing spectacle of the most stylish people in Europe.

The romance of Rome is best experienced through an evening stroll in one of the city's green spaces. If you are not in love already, then looking across the city's tiled roofs and marble domes from the Passeggiata del Gianicolo at sunset, when the sky is streaked with pale reds and oranges, you soon will be. By turns beautiful, brash, theatrical, serene, contradictory, the allure of Rome is impossible to pin down. As the poet Henry Wadsworth Longfellow commented: "There may be other cities that please us for a while, but Rome alone completely satisfies."

VATICAN CITY

At the heart of the Catholic Church, the influence of this tiny fortified territory stretches to all four corners of the globe and its museums contain some of the world's greatest art treasures.

THE VATICAN STATE

Ⓜ *Line A: Ottaviana San Pietro*

Once in St Peter's Square, you've left Italy and are in the Vatican City, bounded on three sides by a large wall. After Italian unification in 1870, the Papal States ceased to exist, and it was not until the 1929 Lateran Treaty that the pope was recognized as sovereign of the independent Vatican State. The pope lives and works in the Papal Palace just off St Peter's Square.

St Peter's Basilica★★★

06 69 88 16 62. www.vatican.va. Inappropriately dressed visitors may be refused access. Closed during Pontifical services.

The first church on this site was built by Constantine in 324 over the tomb of St Peter. The present basilica was begun by Pope Julius II in 1503. Its construction took 120 years and saw the reigns of 20 popes and the supervision of ten different architects, including Bramante, Michelangelo,

and Bernini. The east front was designed by Carlo Maderno, and the pope gives his annual Easter blessing from the balcony beneath the pediment. The porch was also designed by Maderno and features the **"Navicella" mosaic** by Giotto from Constantine's basilica. The enormous space of the interior is beautifully proportioned. The over-all length of the church, including the porch, is about 692ft/211m, and there are 450 statues, 11 chapels, and 45 altars. Most of the internal decoration of St Peter's is the work of Bernini.

Don't miss:
+ **St Peter's Chair★★★** Bernini's throne in sculpted bronze contains the remains of a 4C episcopal chair perhaps used by St Peter. Above is a gilded window with the dove of the Holy Ghost, veiled in clouds.
+ **Clement XIII's Monument ★★★** The fine Neoclassical de-sign by Canova dates from 1792.
+ **Michelangelo's Pietà★★★** This masterpiece, sculpted in 1499–1500 by Michelangelo at the age of 25, can be seen in the Cappella della Pietà.
+ **Urban VIII's Monument★★★** Commissioned from Bernini in 1628, this monument is considered a masterpiece of 17C funerary art.
+ **Paul III's Monument★★★** This monument by Guglielmo della Porta shows the pope with two allegorical statues.

Vatican Inc.

The Vatican State has its own bank, said to be profitable but not immune to controversy, as the Banco Ambrosiano scandal proved. It issues its own euro coins showing the head of the pope, and also issues its own stamps.

- **Alexander VII's Monument★★** Bernini completed this sculpture in 1678, two years before his death. The pope kneels among allegorical statues of Truth, Justice, Charity, and Prudence.
- **Baldacchino★★★** Unveiled by Pope Urban VIII in 1633, Bernini's great bronze canopy (95ft/29m) was criticized by his contemporaries as being too theatrical and in bad taste.
- **Dome★★★** Michelangelo's dome is the largest in the city. From an internal gallery at the base of the dome, you can appreciate the vast dimensions of the basilica. A staircase climbs to a terrace surrounding the lantern 394ft/120m above St Peter's Square.
- **Statue of St Peter★★** Countless pilgrims have kissed the foot of this much revered 13C statue by Arnolfo di Cambio. It is said to have been made out of the bronze statue of Jupiter on the Capitol.
- **Innocent VIII's Monument ★★★** This Renaissance work by Antonio del Pollaiolo is one of the few monuments preserved from the earlier church.

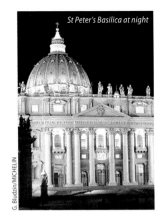

St Peter's Basilica at night

G. Bludzin/MICHELIN

Museo Storico e Tesoro★ – 06 69 88 18 40. Closed Easter, Christmas. €9. The Treasury holds some artifacts from the 4C basilica, as well as sculptures, vestments, and other liturgical objects. The **tomb of Sixtus IV★★★** (1493) by Antonio del Pollaiolo is a masterpiece of bronze sculpture. Junius Bassus's 4C **sarcophagus★★★** was found beneath the basilica and is a remarkable funerary sculpture richly decorated with biblical scenes.

Necropoli Vaticana★★ – *Book well in advance by applying to Ufficio Scavi, http://saintpeters basilica.org/Necropolis/Scavi.htm. Children must be minimum 15 yrs.* This burial ground lies beneath the Vatican and was partly filled in by Constantine to form the basilica's foundations. It comprises tombs dating 1C to early 4C, and that of St Peter, said to contain his relics and to be here because the site is near Nero's circus where he may have died. The Julian family tomb contains the oldest-known Christian mosaics.

Piazza san Pietro★★★ – The square acts as a sort of huge vestibule for the great basilica that dominates the Vatican City, with the curving colonnades on either side like welcoming arms. The square was the work of Bernini under Pope Alexander VII. At the center stands a granite **obelisk** from Heliopolis brought to Rome in AD 37 by Caligula. Sixtus V erected it in St Peter's Square in 1585. The two **fountains** are attributed to Carlo Maderno and Bernini.

VATICAN CITY

25

Vatican Museums★★★

Entrance: Viale Vaticano. 06 69 88 46 76. www.vatican.va. Ticket office: Open 9am–4pm. Skip the queues and book online. Closed Sun (except last Sun every month, no charge 9am–12.30pm), Catholic holy days, and public holidays. Vatican Museums and Sistine Chapel €15.

The fabulous collections of the Vatican are housed in the palaces built by the popes from the 13C onward. The first displays were established by Julius II in 1503, and his successors continued to add to the collections and also commission artworks from some of the greatest Renaissance painters. There are rooms, galleries, and museums to visit, and of course the glorious Sistine Chapel. The **Chariot Room** contains a restored marble **Roman chariot★★** drawn by two horses, the **Gallery of Maps★** has fascinating frescoes of 16C maps, and the **Gallery of Tapestries** has Flemish tapestries first shown in 1531. The **Gallery of the Candelabra** is an 18C loggia, now enclosed, containing fabulous 2C candelabra. The **Carriage Pavilion** exhibits modes of transport from sedan chairs to horse-drawn carriages and automobiles. It is an almost impossible task to pick out the highlights as there are so many.

Egyptian Museum – Founded by pope Gregory XVI, the collection includes antiquities acquired by the popes in the 18C and statues found nearby that had been brought back from Egypt during the Empire or that are Roman copies of 1C–2C works.

Detail of Room of the Borgo Fire

J. Malburet/MICHELIN

Chiaramonti Museum and Lapidary Gallery – The Chiaramonti Museum—set up by Pius VII, whose family name was Chiaramonti—has kept the appearance created by Canova in 1807. It has Roman copies of Greek works, portraits, and funerary monuments. The Lapidary Gallery houses over 3,000 pagan and Christian inscriptions *(open to specialists only)*.

Braccio Nuovo – Built by Pius VII, the New Wing holds Roman sculptures and copies of Greek sculptures, such as the **"Doryphoros,"** a copy of a 5C BC bronze original by Polyclitus, and the statue of **Augustus★★**, a fine example of official Roman art.

Pio-Clementino Museum★★★ – This museum is housed in the Belvedere Palace and Simonetti's 18C extension and is devoted to Greek and Roman art. The internal **courtyard★**, originally on a square plan and planted with orange trees, acquired its octagonal outline when Simonetti added a portico in the 18C.

Highlights:

♦ **The Apoxyomenos★★★**
A statue of an athlete scraping his skin with a strigil, a 1C AD Roman copy of a Greek original by Lysippus (4C BC).

♦ **Laocoön★★★** Unearthed in

Nero's Golden House, this sculpture was the work of a group of artists from Rhodes (1C BC).

- **Apollo★★★** This statue is probably copied from a 4C BC Greek original by a Roman sculptor. It may have held a bow in the left hand and an arrow in the right.
- **Perseus★★** This Neoclassical work by Canova was bought by Pope Pius VII.
- **Hermes★★★** A 2C AD Roman work, inspired by an original Greek bronze, representing the messenger god.
- **The Venus of Cnidos★★** This is a Roman copy of Praxiteles' statue for the sanctuary at Cnidos in Asia Minor (4C BC), which was famous for being the first representation of a goddess in the nude.
- **The Belvedere Torso★★★** The masterly work of the Athenian Apollonius, who lived in Rome in the 1C BC, this expressive torso was much admired by Michelangelo.

Etruscan Museum★ – Founded in 1837 by Gregory XVI, this museum houses objects from southern Etruria, particularly metalwork such as the superb **golden clasp★★**, decorated with lions and ducks. The Bronze Room houses the striking late 5C BC figure **Mars★★** found at Todi. A beautiful **amphora★★★** by Exekias shows heroes Achilles and Ajax. The **Biga Room** has a 1C Roman two-horse **chariot★★** (biga), which was reconstructed in the18C.

Raphael Rooms★★★ – When Julius II became pope in 1503, he arranged to have these four rooms redecorated by a young painter from Urbino. The frescoes that Raphael painted are among the masterpieces of the Renaissance. They were damaged by the troops of Charles V, during the sack of Rome in 1527, but have been restored. The **Room of the Borgo Fire** was the last room painted by Raphael and he only designed the frescoes and some of the cartoons, which were then completed by his assistants. The **Signature Room** was used as a library, a study, and for signing papal bulls and was the first room painted by Raphael. The decorative theme illustrates the principles of Neoplatonic philosophy: Truth, Goodness, and Beauty. The **Heliodorus Room** was the suite's private antechamber and was decorated by Raphael after the Signature Room. The theme here is the divine protection of the Church. The fresco showing *St Peter Delivered from Prison*, with its dramatic lighting, anticipates the genius of Caravaggio and Rembrandt by more than a century. In 1520 Raphael died, and he probably had little to do with the work in the **Hall of Constantine**, which was finished by his followers, led by Giulio Romano and Francesco Penni. The theme of this room is

When in Rome…
The guards are Swiss! To be precise, they must be single Catholic males of Swiss citizenship who have trained with the Swiss military and have an exemplary service record. Responsible for the safety of the pope, the Swiss guards wear traditional Renaissance-style uniform.

VATICAN CITY

27

the triumph of Christianity over paganism. Adjoining these rooms is the **Raphael Loggia★★** *(open to specialists only)*, designed initially by Bramante and then completed by Raphael with paintings representing scenes from the Old and New Testament.

Nicholas V's Chapel★★ – One of the oldest parts of the Vatican Palace, converted into a chapel by Nicholas V and decorated by Fra Angelico. The wall paintings illustrate the lives of St Stephen and St Lawrence and were extensively restored in the 18C and 19C.

Borgia Apartment★ – These rooms of Alexander VI, the Borgia pope, are decorated with frescoes by Pinturicchio. They house the collection of **Modern Religious Art★★**, inaugurated by Paul VI in 1973, including works by Chagall, Gauguin, Klee, Kandinsky, Utrillo, Odilon Redon, Braque, and Moore, and stained glass by Fernand Leger, Jacques Villon, and George Meistermann.

Sistine Chapel★★★ – Named after Pope Sixtus IV, this is the main chapel of the Vatican Palace. It is the venue for the most solemn ceremonies of the Holy See and its dimensions—132ft/40m long,

44ft/13m wide, and 68ft/21m high—are exactly the same as those given in the Bible for Solomon's Temple. The chapel's **walls** feature frescoes by the greatest artists of the 15C and 16C including Perugino, Botticelli, and Ghirlandaio. The paintings show parallel scenes from the lives of Moses and Jesus, showing the human condition before and after the Messiah. In 1508, Michelangelo was called to Rome by Julius II to paint the chapel **ceiling**. The result was one of the greatest works of Western civilization, a masterpiece filled with powerful movement charting the Creation and the Fall. The side panels show the Prophets and heroes of the Old Testament, and the Classical Sibyls who were said to have foreseen the birth of Christ. The work took Michelangelo four years to complete. In 1534 he was commissioned by Paul III to complete the decoration of the chapel with a fresco of **The Last Judgment** above the altar as a warning to the unfaithful. This striking work reflects the turmoil of the Reformation and the artist's own tormented attitude to his faith. The naked bodies writhing in a baleful light startled viewers when it was unveiled, and in the 16C Pius IV had the naked figures clothed by Daniele da Volterra.

Restoring the Sistine Chapel

This vast undertaking, carried out by Italian experts and financed by Japanese patrons, took 18 years to complete. Twelve years (1980–92) were spent on Michelangelo's frescoes. Most of the restoration work consisted of cleaning the frescoes, darkened by dust and candle smoke, with a mixture of bicarbonate of soda and ammonium. After 500 years, Michelangelo's original colors—ranging from bright orange, clear pink, pale green to brilliant yellow and turquoise—sparkle gloriously again.

MUST SEE

Ceiling of the Sistine Chapel

© lexan/iStockphoto.com

Vatican Library★ – Pius V's Chapel displays the varied treasures of the Sancta Sanctorum, the private chapel of the popes in the Lateran Palace. Other rooms and the **Museo Sacra** feature collections of ancient artifacts and early Christian antiquities, as well as medieval treasures. Look out for the **Aldobrandini Marriage Room** where a fresco from the Augustan period depicts wedding preparations.

Pinacoteca★★★ – The Picture Gallery has works dating from the 12C to the high Renaissance. Highlights include the **Stefaneschi Triptych** by Giotto and 15C works by Fra Angelico and Filippo Lippi. One room is entirely devoted to paintings by **Raphael★★★** including his last painting completed shortly before his death in 1520, the *Transfiguration*. Look out for **St Jerome★★** by Leonardo da Vinci and Caravaggio's **Descent from the Cross★★**.

Profane and Christian Museums★ – A fine modern building begun in 1963 contains the Museum of Antique Art assembled by Gregory XVI (1831–46) and the Museum of Christian Art founded in 1854 by Pius IX. Among the important pieces in the Profane Museum are the **Cancelleria Reliefs★★** and the 3C **mosaics★** from the Baths of Caracalla. The Christian Museum has early Christian sculptures and sarcophagi.

Vatican Gardens★★★ – The origins of these extensive and magnificent grounds date back to 1279, when Pope Nicholas III moved his residence from the Lateran Palace to the Vatican and began planting an orchard, lawn, and garden. The fountains and statues are gifts from various countries. A highlight is Pius IV's **Casina**, a charming 16C summerhouse decorated with delightful frescoes, reliefs, and stucco-work.

VATICAN CITY

ANCIENT ROME

With a weathered column or statue around every corner, in Rome ancient history is hard to ignore—a reminder of the time when all roads led to Rome and it was the most powerful city in the world.

THE CAPITOLINE★★★

🅼 *Line B: Colosseo*

Rome's smallest hill is also its most famous. The Capitoline was the city's religious and political center in antiquity, with the temple of Jupiter Capitolinus overlooking the Forum.

🐾 Walking Tour

✕ **Lunch stop** – Capitoline Museums café.

Scalinata d'Aracoeli – In 1348, the plague ravaged Italy but Rome was miraculously spared. The Aracoeli Steps were built as an offering of thanks. From the top there is a fine **view★** of the city.

Santa Maria in Aracoeli★★ – *Open 9am–12.30pm, 2.30–6.30pm.* This church was built on the site of a Greek monastery in 1250 by the Franciscans. It contains several works of art, including tombs by Andrea Bregno, Donatello, and Michelangelo. The floor is one of the best-preserved examples of the work of the Cosmati, 13C Roman marble-workers. The **frescoes★** in the Cappella di San Bernardino da Siena were painted by Pinturicchio. The **Cappella del Santo**

Bambino takes its name from a 15C wooden icon of the Christ-child that was supposed to have miraculous healing powers. At the foot of the Aracoeli Steps is **La Cordonata**, the stepped ramp leading up to the piazza. The two Egyptian lions guarding the entrance were found on the Campus Martius.

Piazza del Campidoglio★★★ – In the Middle Ages the piazza was known as "Monte Caprino" (Goat Hill) and animals grazed among the ruins. In 1536, Pope Paul III commissioned Michelangelo to draw up plans for its restoration. The restored **Statue dei Dioscuri★** show two Roman knights standing beside their horses. The **Trofei di Mario** (Marius's Trophies) is the name given to the sculptures (1C BC) that commemorate Domitian's conquest of the German people.

Palazzo Senatorio★★★ – *Closed to the public; occupied by the offices of the local authority.* In 1143, the Roman people set up the Commune. The Senate was created to lead the government and met in this palace that was built over the ruins of the **Tabularium** (*see Major Museums, Capitoline Museums★★★*).

About turn
Michelangelo was making a symbolic gesture when he turned the orientation of the Piazza del Campidoglio around to face the modern city and papal Rome rather than the Forum and the past.

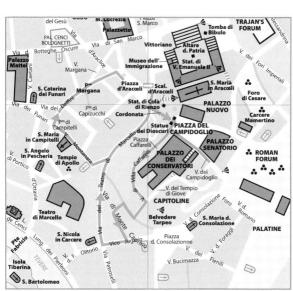

Palazzo dei Conservatori and Palazzo Nuovo★★★ – This matching pair of elegant palaces house the **Capitoline Museums★★★** *(see Major Museums)*. The **Rupe Tarpea** (Tarpeian Rock), from which traitors were traditionally thrown during the Republic, can be seen from Via della Consolazione. *(Visitors should exercise caution in this sometimes unsavory area.)*

Teatro di Marcello★★ – The Theater of Marcellus was begun by Julius Caesar and completed by Augustus. Holding 15,000 spectators, it was the second-largest theater in Rome after Pompey's in the Campus Martius. It was damaged by fire in AD 64 and was abandoned early in the 4C. In the 16C, the noble Savelli family turned it into a palace, the remains of which are visible today above the old arches.

Tempio di Apollo Sosiano★★ – The first temple to Apollo was raised on this site in the 5C BC. In 34 BC, Caius Sosius, governor of Cilicia and Syria, rebuilt the sanctuary and it became known as the **Temple of Apollo Sosianus**. The three elegant fluted **columns★★** belonged to the temple's porch.

Santa Maria in Campitelli – The **interior★** of this 17C church by Carlo Rainaldi is a forest of columns. Along Via dei Delfini is **Piazza Margana**, a charming square among narrow medieval streets. Farther along, **Piazza d'Aracoeli** features a fountain by Giacomo della Porta.

31

ANCIENT ROME

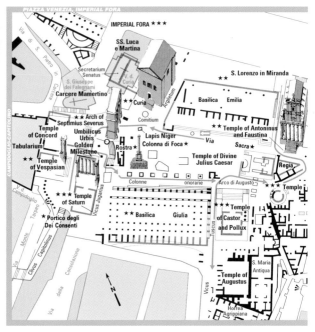

PIAZZA VENEZIA, IMPERIAL FORA

IMPERIAL FORA ★★★

SS. Luca e Martina

Secretarium Senatus
S. Giuseppe dei Falegnami
Carcere Mamertino

V. d. Curia

S. Lorenzo in Miranda

★★ Curia

Argiletum

Basilica Emilia

Comitium

★★ Arch of Septimius Severus
Temple of Concord
Umbilicus Urbis
Golden Milestone
Tabularium
★★ Temple of Vespasian

Lapis Niger
Colonna di Foca ★
Rostra ★

★★ Temple of Antoninus and Faustina

Via Sacra ★

Temple of Divine Julius Caesar

★★★ Temple of Saturn

Colonne onorarie

Arco di Augusto

★★★ Temple

Regia

★★ Temple of Castor and Pollux

Portico degli Dei Consenti

★★ Basilica Giulia

Vicus Jugarius
Vicus Tuscus

Clivus Capitolinus

S. Maria Antiqua

Temple of Augustus

Horrea Agrippiana

THE ROMAN FORUM★★★

Ⓜ Line B: Colosseo. Entrance on Via dei Fori Imperiali. 06 39 96 77 00. www.pierreci.it. Open daily 8.30am–7.15pm (last admission 6.15pm). Closed Jan 1, May 1, Christmas. €9 (includes access to the Colosseum and Palatine).

Today the Forum is a mass of crumbled walls and columns populated by stray cats and tourists, but in ancient times it was the bustling hub of the city where all kinds of Romans, from slaves to senators, went about their everyday business. It was the chosen site for monuments and temples dedicated to emperors deified after their death. It is overlooked by the Palatine Hill, where today umbrella pines shade the husks of aristocratic houses.

ꙮ Walking Tour

Basilica Emilia – Built in 179 BC and frequently restored, this building housed business transactions and judicial hearings, as well as citizens' meetings. Along the south side there was a line of shops opening into a portico. The main hall was divided by two rows of colored marble columns with a finely carved marble entablature.

Via Sacra★ – Victorious generals would process along the Sacred Way to the Capitoline to thank Jupiter for his protection. The **Argiletum**, one of the busiest streets in Rome, separated the Basilica Emilia from the Curia and led to Suburra, a slum district. Sections of travertine paving remain.

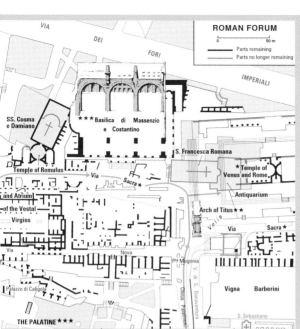

ROMAN FORUM

0   50 m

—— Parts remaining
—— Parts no longer remaining

VIA
DEI
FORI
IMPERIALI

SS. Cosma
e Damiano

★★★Basilica di Massenzio
e Costantino

S. Francesca Romana

Temple of Romulus

Via

Sacra ★

★Temple of
Venus and Rome

Antiquarium

and Atrium

of the Vestal
Virgins

Arch of Titus★★

Via   Sacra ★

Via

Velia

Nova

Pte Mugonia

Palazzo di Caligola

CLIVUS Palatinus

v. di S. Bonaventura

Vigna   Barberini

S. Sebastiano

THE PALATINE ★★★

THE PALATINE

Curia★★ – The first Curia (where the senate met) in the Republican period was more or less on the site of the chancel of Santi Luca e Martina. The restored brick building visible today is on the site of Caesar's Curia, built in the 1C BC and remodeled by Diocletian in the 3C. The original structure had a marble façade surmounted by a tympanum covered in travertine; the bronze door was removed to St John Lateran by Alexander VII in the 17C. At the far end of the Curia there are traces of the pedestal of the golden **Statue of Victory** erected by Octavian in 29 BC to mark his defeat of Antony and Cleopatra. For over three centuries, the emperors worshiped the statue, burning incense on the altar, but when Christianity became the official religion Emperor Gratian removed it, and its fate is unknown. **Trajan's Plutei★★** are two sculpted panels found in the Forum and probably commissioned by Trajan or his successor Hadrian to decorate the Rostra. The **Lapis Niger** (Black Stone) was believed by the ancients to mark the tomb of Romulus.

Rostra★ – During the Republican period this orators' platform stood between the Lapis Niger and the present Curia. The remains seen today are those of the Rostra moved in 44 BC by Julius Caesar. The **Arch of Septimius Severus★★** was built in 203 and is topped by statues of the emperor, his two sons (Caracalla and Geta), and the figure of Victory. The 3C circular

33

temple, the **Umbilicus Urbis** marked the symbolic center of the city. The **Golden Milestone**, a marble column, covered with gilded bronze, displayed the distances between Rome and the Empire's major cities.

Temple of Vespasian★★ – Three elegant columns, excavated in 1811, are still standing; they formed a corner of the temple built by Titus and Domitian to honor their dead father. Above the architrave is a decorative frieze. Nearby is the **Temple of Concord**, built to celebrate reconciliation between the patricians and the plebeians, and the **Tabularium** built in 78 BC to house the state records, including some bronze tablets of the old Roman laws. The podium and a few remaining pillars form the base of the Senatorial Palace. The use of peperine, a very simple building material, and the Doric order typify the austerity of Republican architecture.

Temple of Saturn★★★ – From 497 onward, a temple dedicated to Saturn stood on this site. Restored several times under the Republic, the temple was then rebuilt in the 4C after a fire. The eight columns of the pronaos that remain date from this period; the travertine podium goes back to the 1C BC. The basement housed the state treasury, administered by the Senate. Behind it is the **Portico degli Dei Consenti★**, best viewed from the Capitoline Hill. These 12 Corinthian columns were reconstructed in 1858. The portico was built by Domitian in honor of the 12 gods in the Roman pantheon, whose statues stood in pairs.

House of the Vestal Virgins

J. Malburet/MICHELIN

Basilica Giulia★★ – In 55 BC, Julius Caesar began building this huge basilica, 340ft/110m long and 130ft/40m wide. Caesar was murdered before the basilica was finished, and it was completed by Augustus. Opposite is the **Colonna di Foca★**, erected in AD 608 to honor the eastern Emperor Phocas who gave the Pantheon to Pope Boniface IV to convert into a church. This is one of the few monuments to have remained standing since the day it was built.

Temple of Divine Julius Caesar – This temple was consecrated by Octavian in 29 BC to the deified Julius Caesar on the site where his body was cremated after his murder in 44 BC. Almost nothing is left of this building except traces of a round altar in a semicircular recess at ground level.

Temple of Castor and Pollux★★★ – This early 5C temple honored Castor and Pollux, known as "the Dioscuri," twin brothers of Clytemnestra and Helen of Troy. The chief remains are three columns supporting an architrave fragment that date from a reconstruction undertaken in the Augustan era. The very high podium, the large Corinthian capitals, and the use of white marble combine to majestic effect. The 6C church of **Santa Maria Antiqua** *(closed for restoration at the time of going to press; 06 48 02 01)* contains paintings dating from the Byzantine period.

Temple and Atrium of the Vestal Virgins★★★ – The cult of Vesta, the goddess of fire, goes back to Numa Pompilius (715–672 BC). The first temple here was built in the 6C BC; this reconstruction from the foundation and the few marble fragments that survived is of the 4C AD temple, which was surrounded by a portico supported on 20 fluted Corinthian columns. The *cella* housed an altar where the fire was kept burning constantly. Next to the temple was the **house of the Vestal Virgins**, the priestesses who officiated in the cult. This was a large two-story building enclosing a courtyard with two pools and a garden. Some of the statues of the Vestals have been placed in the courtyard.

Temple of Antoninus and Faustina★★ – Emperor Antoninus Pius erected this huge temple to his wife, Faustina, on her death in AD 141. When Antoninus himself died, in AD 161, the Senate decided to dedicate the temple to both husband and wife. The beautiful monolithic columns of the pronaos still stand in situ on their high podium. The frieze of griffins and candelabra on the entablature is a masterpiece of craftsmanship. In the 11C the church of

San Lorenzo in Miranda was established in the ruins; the current building dates from 1602. The **Temple of Romulus** is thought to be dedicated to the son of Emperor Maxentius, who died in 307. Dating from the early 4C, the construction is circular and flanked by two rooms with apses. In the 6C, the temple became a vestibule to the church of Santi Cosma e Damiano. It retains the original 4C **bronze doors★**.

Santi Cosma e Damiano – *Open 9am–1pm, 3–5pm.* This 6C basilica on Via dei Fori Imperiali was established in what had been the library of Vespasian's Forum. The beautiful 17C coffered **ceiling★** shows the triumph of St Cosmas and St Damian. The church also has fine Byzantine **mosaics★** on the chancel arch and the apse.

Basilica di Massenzio e Costantino★★★ – Maxentius was proclaimed emperor in 305, and constructed this basilica, the last to be built in Rome. Built of brick beneath a groined vault, it was rectangular and divided into three by huge pillars flanked by columns. When Constantine took the throne in 312 he completed the basilica, moving the entrance to the façade overlooking the Via Sacra and adding a portico of four porphyry columns.

Temple of Venus and Rome★ – Built between AD 121 and136 by Hadrian, it was the largest temple in Rome and designed in the Greek style with steps on all sides. It was surrounded by a colonnade and had two *cellae* with apses back to back, one dedicated to the goddess

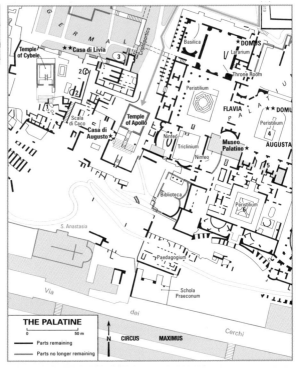

THE PALATINE

0 ——— 50 m

N CIRCUS MAXIMUS

Parts remaining
Parts no longer remaining

Rome, the other to Venus. The part of the temple facing the Forum was incorporated into the 8C church of **Santa Francesca Romana** *(open 10am–noon, 4–7pm)*. The 12C Romanesque **bell tower★** is one of the most elegant in Rome and the church has a beautiful 17C coffered ceiling. Attached to the church is the **Antiquarium**, a museum of artifacts found in the Forum from the earliest period of ancient Rome.

Arch of Titus★★ – This triumphal arch was erected after Titus's death in AD 81 to commemorate his capture of Jerusalem in AD 70. The single archway was restored by Luigi Valadier in 1821. The two

low **reliefs** under the vault are among the masterpieces of Roman sculpture and show soldiers carrying off the booty pillaged from the temple in Jerusalem. To the right the **Clivus Palatinus** leads up **the Palatine**. This road follows the hollow between the two peaks: the Palatium to the left, the Germalus to the right. The rectangular ditch marks the site of **Domitian's Arch**. The sections of high brick wall facing down the hill belonged to the portico of the Domus Flavia. The path emerges at the top of the hill on the artificial plateau created when Domitian filled in the hollow between the Palatium and the Germalus.

Domus Flavia★ – This was the center of official imperial activity. It is still possible to visualize how the building would have looked. There were three rooms behind the portico: the **Lararium**, the emperor's private chapel; the enormous **Throne Room**; and the **Basilica**, where the emperor dispensed justice. Behind these three rooms is a courtyard (**Peristilium**) originally surrounded by a portico, traces of which remain. Beyond the peristyle is the **Triclinium**, the dining room, which was certainly the most beautiful room in the palace; part of the colored marble floor has been preserved. The **underground rooms★** are all that remain of houses from the Republican era and of Nero's structures when they were buried under Domitian's building projects. The **Museo Palatino★★★** is housed in a former convent built over the ruins of Domitian's Imperial Palace, and contains articles and fragments found on the Palatine.

Domus Augustana★★ – This was the official imperial residence, and even in ruins gives an impression of grandeur and luxury. Four rooms of splendid and painstakingly restored 30 BC frescoes were opened to the public in 2008. To the left is the **Stadium★**, possibly designed to stage private games and spectacles for Domitian.

Casa di Augusto★ – This is believed to have been the original house of Gaius Julius Caesar Octavianus before he became Rome's first emperor. The **Temple of Apollo** was probably built by Augustus; the podium and a column of the pronaos are recognizable.

Casa di Livia★★ – The home of Augustus and his third wife Livia. One of the best-preserved buildings on the Palatine, it contains delightful frescoes.

Temple of Cybele – The remains of this date from the time of Augustus. The arches facing the temple belonged to the rear façade of Tiberius's Palace. In front of the temple are the so-called **huts of Romulus** (*closed for restoration at the time of going to press*). The position of the 9C BC huts is indicated by the holes for the posts that would have supported them. They are the earliest traces of the city.

Cryptoportico – This network of underground passages dates from Nero's reign and linked the various Imperial buildings. Legend has it that the Emperor Caligula was murdered in one of the passages.

Orti Farnesiani – *Closed for restoration at the time of going to press.* These 16C gardens were laid out by Cardinal Alexander Farnese. A series of terraces rise up the north face of the Palatine and on the top of the hill.

Livia Drusilla (58BC–AD29)
Livia's reputation for having had a number of her family "taken care of" in order that her son Tiberius might become emperor has been handed down over the years. However, she is also said to have played the role of dutiful wife and was married to Augustus for over 50 years.

IMPERIAL FORA★★★

Line B: Colosseo or Cavour

Crowded with souvenir stalls and tourists, and bisected by Mussolini's Via dei Fori Imperiali, there are still glimpses here of the bustling administrative and commercial center of the ancient city.

✿⸙ Walking Tour

✕ **Lunch stop** – Via Cavour.

Santi Luca e Martina – This 7C church was dedicated to Martina, who had been martyred under Septimius Severus. From 1588, it also honored St Luke. In the 17C Cardinal Francesco Barberini commissioned Pietro da Cortona to build a new shrine above the old one. Da Cortona designed a beautiful **façade★**, reminiscent of the style of Borromini.

Foro di Nerva – Begun by Domitian, this forum was completed by Nerva in 98. Very little remains of the long and narrow complex, traversed by the Argiletum, a street linking the Roman Forum with the Suburra district. The **Temple of Minerva** stood here, but its ruins were demolished early in the 17C. By the east wall stand two beautiful **columns★** and some fragments of a frieze that adorned the wall enclosing the forum. Next to Nerva's Forum was the **Forum of Vespasian**, built from 71–75. It formed a square and extended roughly from the Basilica di Massenzio e Costantino to the Torre de Conti. In the south corner was a library, now occupied by the church of Santi Cosima e Damiano.

Carcere Mamertino – *06 67 92 902. Guided tour (10min). Open 9am–7pm (summer 6pm). Donations welcome.* The Mamertine was the Roman state prison; it consists of two rooms, one above the other, hollowed out of the Capitoline beneath the church of San Giuseppe dei Falegnami (St Joseph of the Carpenters). In the Middle Ages, a legend arose that St Peter had been imprisoned here, hence the name of the adjoining street.

Foro di Cesare★★ – For his forum, Caesar chose a central posi-

Trajan's Market

P. Orain/Michelin

tion at the foot of the Capitoline. It cost 60 million sestercii to clear the site, according to Cicero, money that came from Caesar's conquest of Gaul (58–51 BC). This forum was rectangular and extended from the Curia to Via di San Pietro in Carcere. About two-thirds of Caesar's forum has been uncovered; the rest is beneath Via dei Fori Imperiali. Three richly sculpted standing columns belonged to the **Temple of Venus Genitrix** and date from the time of Domitian and Trajan. Caesar claimed that his family descended from Venus through her son, Aeneas. The edge of the forum was lined with shops, still visible beneath the Clivus Argentarius. During Trajan's reign, a portico was added down the long side nearest the Clivus Argentarius. Its two long rows of granite columns still remain. It has been identified as the **Basilica Argentaria**, where the money changers plied their trade.

Imperial Fora★★★ – As the Roman Forum grew too small to accommodate the business of the city, the emperors built new meeting places to the north. Quarried and pillaged during the medieval era and the Renaissance, the Imperial Fora disappeared under new buildings. The Fascists cleared the area for military parades, leveling the Velian Hill and paving **Via dei Fori Imperiali** right through the area. Pedestrians can stroll here on Sundays, when the road is closed to traffic until 6pm.

Trajan's Forum★★★ – Visitors enter the Forum at Largo Romolo e Remo. The Visitor Center dei Fori Imperiali (in front of the Basilica dei Santi Cosma e Damiano) organizes tours and audio guides and provides brochures. 06 67 97 702. Open Tue–Sun 9.30am–7.30pm. Closed Mon, Jan 1, Jun 2, Christmas. Trajan's Forum was inaugurated in 113. Its construction involved work on a huge scale, including the cutting back and leveling of a spur of the Quirinal, which extended toward the Capitoline. Trajan financed the forum with the proceeds from his war with the Dacians, who lived in what is now Romania. Trajan's was the largest of the imperial fora and certainly the most beautiful. The entrance was set in a slightly curved wall facing southeast. The apse of the northeast wall is still visible, running parallel with the concave façade of the market and marked by two columns, one of which remains. The **Basilica Ulpia**, named after Trajan's family, had five aisles, a marble floor, and two storys of marble and granite columns, some of which are still standing. Beyond lay two public libraries (biblioteca): one contained Greek works, the other Latin manuscripts and Trajan's personal records. Between the two was a courtyard with Trajan's Column at its center. In the middle of the forum stood an equestrian statue in gilded bronze of the emperor.

Trajan's Column★★★ – Designed by Apollodorus of Damascus, the column stands about 125ft/38m high and consists of 17 marble drums. Sculpted scenes from Trajan's campaigns against the Dacians spiral upward, and a set of replica casts are kept in the **Museo della Civiltà Romana★★**. The size of the panels and the figures increases toward the top of the column, which was originally brilliantly colored. A bronze statue of Trajan stood on top, but it was replaced with a statue of St Peter by Pope Sixtus V. Although a pagan monument, Trajan's Column was never damaged by the Christians, who believed that the emperor's soul had been saved by the prayers of St Gregory. Inside, there is a spiral staircase (*closed to the public*), lit by windows in the decorative panels.

Trajan's Market★★ – *Via IV Novembre 94; during restoration the entrance is on Piazza Madonna di Loreto, near Trajan's Column. 06 06 06 08. http://en.mercatiditraiano.it. Site partially closed for restoration at the time of going to press. Open Tue–Sun 9am–7pm, 9am–2pm. Closed, Jan 1, May 1.* As well as being a shopping center, the market was used for the division and redis-

tribution of supplies, administered by the imperial authorities. There is a magnificent vaulted room where civil servants may have worked.
Via Biberatica★ serves the upper part of the market, which is lined with well-preserved shops and houses. The tiered **façade** demonstrates the genius of architect Apollodorus of Damascus, who gave a monumental appearance to this utilitarian complex. The shallow shops on the ground floor opened directly onto the street. The original paving remains, curving from the Torre del Grillo to the Via IV Novembre. The **Museo dei Fori Imperiali** in the old market buildings displays artifacts uncovered in recent digs.

Torre delle Milizie★ – *Entrance from Trajan's Market. 06 67 90 048. Open Mar–Oct Tue–Sun 9am–7pm (Nov–Feb 5pm). Closed Jan 6, Easter,*

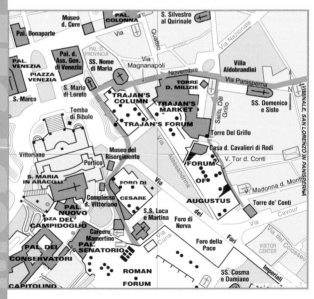

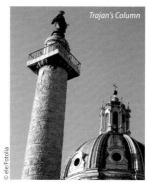

Trajan's Column

© ele/Fotolia

Apr 25, May 1, Jun 29, Aug 15 and Christmas. One of the best-preserved buildings of medieval Rome, this was the keep of a 13C castle built by Pope Gregory IX. The tower leans slightly because of an earthquake in the 14C; it has lost its top story and crenelations. From Via IV Novembre, there is a view of the trees in the public gardens of the **Villa Aldobrandini** and the Baroque façade of the church of **Santi Domenico e Sisto**, completed in 1655.

Forum of Augustus★★ – This was begun in 31 BC, after a considerable amount of demolition work. The site extended from the old Forum to the edge of the unsavory Suburra district, from which it was isolated by a high wall. The two sides facing southeast and northwest bowed into two semicircles, which are still visible. Against the center of the back wall stood the **Temple of Mars Ultor**, which was approached by a majestic flight of steps. A few columns to the front and side remain. Members of the imperial family came here for the ceremony of the *toga virilis*, a rite of manhood that took place at about age 17, when a boy would put aside the toga that he had worn until then and first put on the white toga of a man. On either side of the temple were two basilicas, in front of the semicircular recesses. Two flights of steps flanked the temple and linked the Forum of Augustus with Suburra. Tiberius later erected two commemorative arches, one on each side of the temple, in honor of Drusus and Germanicus, who pacified Germany and Pannonia, in present-day Eastern Europe.

Casa dei Cavalieri di Rodi – *06 67 89 261. Open Tue Thu 10am–1pm. Closed Aug and public holidays. Guided tours only (45min). Apply at least 2 weeks in advance to the Ufficio Monumenti medievali e moderni Mon–Fri 9am–1pm.* Since the 12C the Knights of Rhodes have had their priory in this house over part of the Forum of Augustus. In the 15C it was built and some of the windows show that Venetian craftsmen were employed. The beautiful 15C loggia overlooking Trajan's Forum is supported by Roman columns. Via Tor de' Conti skirts the imposing wall that separated Augustus's Forum from the Suburra district. The **Arco dei Pentani** marked the entrance to the forum. At the end of the street is the imposing sight of the 13C **Torre de' Conti**. **Via Madonna dei Monti** leads through what was once the sleazy ancient Suburra district, now lively with craft shops. Via Panisperna crosses the **Viminale**, one of the seven hills of Rome, and ends in the tree-lined courtyard of the church of **San Lorenzo in Panisperna**, a tiny oasis from another era.

THE AVENTINE★

Ⓜ *Line B: Circo Massimo*

This pleasant residential district is dotted with magnificent villas and religious houses, as well as a number of Paleochristian churches. In the Republican era the Aventine was a stronghold of the plebeians.

⚬⚬Walking Tour

✕ **Lunch stop** – Viale Aventino.

Circo Massimo – This was the largest circus in Rome and was used exclusively for chariot races. The track (more than 550yd/500m long) was bordered by banks of seats. In the 4C BC, the arena was divided by a central reservation, called the *spina*, which linked the two conical turning posts *(metae)*. In the Augustan era, an obelisk (now in the **Piazza del Popolo★★**) more than 75ft/23m high was erected on the *spina* and a splendid stand was built for the emperor and his family. At this time the Circus Maximus could accommodate 150,000 spectators. Later emperors continued to enlarge it and make improvements. The few remains near the Porta Capena belong to Trajan's period. The little tower here dates from the Middle Ages; it was part of a fortress built by the noble Frangipani family. From the **Piazzale Ugo la Malfa** there is a **view★** of the semicircular façade of the Domus Augustana on the Palatine. In the square stands a **Monument to Giuseppe Mazzini**, a writer and politician who was instrumental in the movement for Italian unification.

Santa Prisca – *06 57 43 798. Open 8am–6pm (Jul 7pm).* This is one of the first places of Christian worship in Rome. Though built in the 17C and 18C, its origins go back to the 2C. Excavations have uncovered a late 2C *mithraeum*, a cave-like shrine *(access from the south aisle of the church)*. Nearby is a twin-nave building, which may

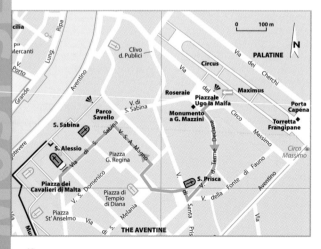

Nave of Santa Sabina

©Britta Jaschinski/APA Publications

have been an earlier Christian structure *(open 2nd and 4th Sun of the month 4pm; €5)*. Traces of buildings dating from the late 1C and early 2C have also been found nearby; they may belong to Trajan's residence.

Parco Savello – Better known as the **Giardino degli Aranci**, this park hugs the apse of Santa Sabina. The northwest side, high above the river, offers a fine **view★**.

Santa Sabina★★ – *06 57 43 573. Open 7am–12.30pm; 3.30pm– 6.30pm. Cloisters and gardens open by appointment only. Minimum donation €1.* This 5C church was transformed in the 16C by Sixtus V and his architect Domenico Fontana, and subsequent Baroque additions hid its medieval character. Extensive restoration has now revived its glory. A beautiful **door★★** of cypress wood belonging to the original church gives access to the nave—its carved panels show scenes from the Old and New Testaments. The **interior★★** has a basilical plan, with a nave and two aisles separated by two rows

of Corinthian columns supporting a light arcade. The frieze of tessellated marble above the arches in the nave dates from the 5C. The rich marble decor of the chancel, dating from the 9C and destroyed by Sixtus V, has been reconstructed from fragments of the original. The 17C chapel dedicated to St Catherine of Siena has been preserved; its multicolored marbles, frescoes, and painted dome clash with the serenity of the rest of the church.

Sant'Alessio – *Open 8.30am– 12.30pm, 3.30–6.30pm.* Legend says that St Alexis was the son of a patrician family, who set out for the Holy Land as a beggar, returning to Rome to die. The story goes that tragically his family did not recognize him and he spent his last days living beneath the staircase of his father's house.

Piazza dei Cavalieri di Malta – This charming square named after the Knights of Malta was designed by Piranesi in the 18C. The priory at no. 3 is famous for the **view★** of St Peter's through the bronze keyhole of its front door.

TESTACCIO★

Ⓜ *Line B: Piramide*

This was ancient Rome's wharf zone, where goods were unloaded and stored. Later it became a slaughterhouse and meat-packing district, and it retains a down-to-earth blue-collar atmosphere.

⌖ Walking Tour

✕ **Lunch stop** – Piazza Testaccio.

Piramide di Caio Cestio★ – Caius Cestius, praetor and tribune of the people, who died in 12 BC, devised Rome's most original mausoleum. The marble pyramid testifies to the grandeur of the Augustan era, when a citizen could erect a tomb worthy of a pharaoh. Nearby is the **Porta San Paolo★**. Once part of the 3C Aurelian Wall, this gate was originally called the **Porta Ostiensis**; it opened into Via Ostiense, which led to St Paul's Basilica—hence the medieval name. **Via Ostiense** dates from the 4C BC; it was one of the most important commercial routes in antiquity.

Centrale Montemartini★★ – *Close to the General Market on Via Ostiense, not far from the Pyramid. 06 57 48 030. www.centralemonte martini.org. Open Tue–Sun 9am– 7pm (Dec 24 and 31 2pm). Closed Jan 1, May 1, Christmas. €4.20 (€8.30 ticket with the Capitoline Museums).* This was Italy's first public thermo-electric power station, and the steam turbines and diesel engines are still an impressive sight. The power station was closed in the 1950s, and restoration began in the early 1990s, when the structure became a multimedia center. It now houses sculptures from the **Capitoline Museums★★★**, which create an interesting contrast between ancient art and industrial archeology. Notable are the group

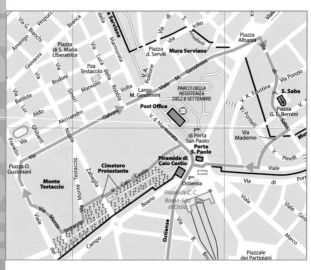

of **Heracles and Athena** (6C BC), which once adorned the Temple of Fortune and Mater Matuta in the sacred precinct of Sant'Omobono; the **Togato Barberini** and statues of his ancestors; two images of **Athena** that face each other in the Machinery Room on the first floor; and in the Steam Room: **Winged Victory**, a 5C BC Greek statue from the Gardens of Sallust, the beautiful **Esquiline Venus★★**, and the **Seated Girl★★** from the Gardens of Licinius.

Returning to the Piazza Ostiensa, the Aventine district **Post Office** (Ufficio Postale) in Via della Marmorata is a fine example of Italian rationalist architecture, designed by A. Libera and M. de Renzi.

Cimitero Protestante – *Via Caio Cestio 6. 06 57 41 900. www.protestantcemetery.it. Open daily 9am–5pm (Sun 1pm). Tours available (pre-booking required). Donations welcome.* Also known as the **Testaccio Cemetery** and **Cimitero Acattolico**, a more appropriate name since the criterion for burial here was "not Catholic," the Protestant Cemetery is the last resting place of many famous people: John Keats and his friend Joseph Severn, Percy Bysshe Shelley, and Axel Munthe, the psychiatrist and author of *The Story of San Michele*. One of the most poignant monuments is the *Angel of Grief* by American sculptor William Story, who died not long after completing this memorial for his wife, and was buried beside her.

Testaccio – The main attraction of this working-class neighborhood is **Monte Testaccio**, some

G. Bludzin/MICHELIN

Industrial architecture and Classical sculpture in the Centrale Montemartini

115ft/35m high, which is formed of the smashed remains of ancient amphorae. Excavations have uncovered several "grottoes," some of which appear to be ancient restaurants and nightspots.

Piazza Albania – In this piazza, near Via Sant'Anselmo, are the remains of the 6C BC **Servian Wall** (Mura Serviane). This part was probably rebuilt in the 1C BC.

San Saba★ – This church is on the site of a 7C oratory for Palestinian monks who had fled from the invading Arabs. The present church dates from the 10C and is dedicated to St Sabas, who founded the original monastery. Although the building underwent various alterations, it was restored in the early 20C. The portico is contemporary with the church, but the columns have been replaced with thick pillars. In the 15C, a single story topped by a loggia was built above the portico. The lack of uniformity between the pillars is typical of medieval buildings, which recycled chunks of ancient sculpture. An unusual feature is the additional aisle on the east side of the church; it probably linked the church to the monastery of the Eastern monks.

THE COLOSSEUM★★★

Ⓜ *Line B: Colosseo*

One of the most famous buildings in the world, the Colosseum is a magnificent symbol of Rome's grandeur. To the south is the peaceful medieval atmosphere of Rome's greenest hill, the Caelian.

☙ Walking Tour

✕ **Lunch stop** – Via delle Terme di Tito.

Colosseum★★★ – *06 39 96 77 00. www.pierreci.it. Open summer 8.30am–7.15pm; winter 8.30am–5.30pm (last admission 1hr before closing time). Closed Jan 1, Christmas. €9 (combined ticket with Palatine Hill and its museums) €20 for a "Roma archeologica" card, valid for 9 archeological sites.* The Colosseum dominates the flat southeast end of the Forum. Vespasian began the construction in AD 72 and the stadium was inaugurated by his son Titus in AD 80 with an extravaganza of races and gladiatorial contests that lasted for 100 days. The stone blocks for the building were brought from the quarries at Albulae, near Tivoli, along specially built roads. Doric, Ionic, and Corinthian columns support three tiers of arcades. The *cavea*, the terraces, began 13ft/4m above the arena. Places were allotted according to social status, with prime spots reserved for the emperor and his suite, and for the Prefect of Rome and the magistrates. Women sat at the top under a colonnade; slaves stood on the terrace above. The Colosseum probably had 45,000 seats and standing space for some 5,000 spectators. Below the arena was a warren of passages and cells where animals waited before being brought to the surface by a series of ramps and lifts. In the 13C, the Frangipani family turned the Colosseum into a fortress, and in the 15C, it became a quarry for builders working on the Palazzo Venezia, Palazzo della Cancelleria, and St Peter's Basilica. Benedict XIV stopped this in the 18C by consecrating the building to the Christian martyrs thought to have perished here, though in fact no Christians were ever killed in the Colosseum.

Arch of Constantine★★★ –

This triumphal arch was built in 315, three years after Constantine's victory over his rival Maxentius at the Milvian Bridge. The design of the two faces is identical, and many of the sculptures were taken from 2C monuments to Trajan, Hadrian, and Marcus Aurelius. Like the Colosseum, the arch eventually merged into medieval fortifications. The **Meta Sudans** nearby, built by Titus and repaired by Constantine, is a fountain in the

Colosseum

B. Morandi/MICHELIN

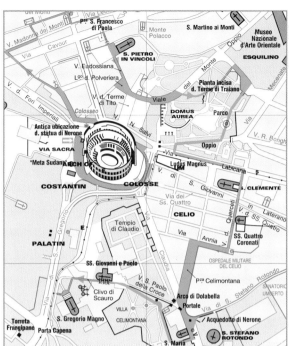

form of a cone of porous stone
that oozed water. This unusual
waterwork marked the turning
point in Roman triumphal proces-
sions, when a general entered the
Via Sacra.

**San Pietro in Vincoli (St Peter
in Chains)**★ – *Open 7am–12.30pm,
3–6pm.* This church to the north of
the Colosseum was consecrated
in the 5C by Sixtus III, although it
probably stands on a much older
construction. The porch was added
in the 15C, and the medieval
interior was altered in the 17C and
18C when the nave was vaulted
and painted with frescoes. The
Mausoleum of Julius II was commissioned by the pope himself in

1505 as a grandiose memorial that
would dominate the center of St
Peter's Basilica. Michelangelo was
appointed to sculpt the statues,
but after spending eight months
in Carrara choosing marble, he
returned to find that the pope had
lost interest. After Julius's death in
1513, the project languished and
Michelangelo sculpted only the
Slaves (now in Florence and Paris)
and the huge seated figure of
Moses★★★. **St Peter's Chains**,
which were supposed to have
shackled the saint in the Mamertine prison, lie in the *confessio*
beneath the chancel. The **crypt**
(closed to the public) is visible
through the grill in the *confessio*.
A fine 4C sarcophagus conserves

47

Basilica dei Santi Giovanni e Paolo

©Juergen Schonnop/Dreamstime.com

the relics of the Maccabees, seven brothers whose martyrdom is recounted in the Old Testament. The nearby **Piazza San Francesco di Paola** is dominated by the former Borgia Palace, the residence of Vanozza Caetani, mother of Cesare and Lucrezia Borgia.

Domus Aurea★★ – *Entrance in Viale Domus Aurea, behind the Colle Oppio gardens. 06 39 96 77 00. www.pierreci.it. Open only for pre-booked visits.* The **Golden House** was built by Nero after the fire that destroyed large parts of Rome in AD 64. The vestibule was on the Velia (where the **Arch of Titus**★★ stands) and contained the famous statue of Nero; the rooms were on the Oppian Hill. In the hollow between, now occupied by the Colosseum, was a vast lake, and all around were gardens and vineyards. After Nero's suicide in AD 68, his successors made efforts to obliterate all traces of his decadent palace. The upper part of the house was razed and the remainder lumped into foundations for the Baths of Titus and Trajan, and the remains of the Golden House were not rediscovered until the

Renaissance. Beneath the ruins of **Trajan's Baths** (Terme di Traiano) several rooms of the palace are open to the public, decorated with frescoes of landscapes and mythological scenes.

Basilica di San Clemente★★
see Major Churches

Santi Quattro Coronati – In the Middle Ages, the church of the **Four Crowned Saints** was part of a fortress that protected the Lateran Palace. The 4C church lasted until 1084, when it was destroyed by Robert Guiscard's troops. A much smaller church was built by Paschal II in the 12C. The identity of the four martyrs, whose sarcophagi are in the 4C crypt, is not certain. The delightful **cloisters**★ were added in the 13C. The 13C **chapel of St Sylvester**★ *(entrance beneath the portico in the inner courtyard; key available in the convent entrance on the north side of the inner court)* has remarkable frescoes, very naive in execution, showing the legend of Pope Sylvester curing Emperor Constantine's leprosy and converting him to Christianity.

Arco di Dolabella – The 1C Arch of Dolabella carries the remains of **Acquedotto di Nerone** (Nero's Aqueduct), which supplied water to the Palatine Hill from the Porta Maggiore.

Santo Stefano Rotondo★ – *06 70 45 11 91/92 or 06 39 96 77 00. Open 9am–12.30pm, 3–5pm.* Built on the Caelian Hill in the late 4C to early 5C, this church was dedicated to St Stephen by the pope at the end of the 5C. The unusual round plan was inspired by the church of the Holy Sepulchre in Jerusalem. The central area was circled by concentric passageways with Ionic supporting columns, though the outer passageway was demolished in the 15C, and a new outer wall built. In the 16C, Niccolò Pomarancio painted 34 frescoes of martyrdom.

Santa Maria in Domnica – *Open 9am–12.30pm, 4.30–7pm.* This church, a favorite for weddings, was founded in the 7C, and greatly altered during the Renaissance. The façade and elegant, round-arched porch were restored in the 16C at the request of Pope Leo X by Andrea Sansovino. The interior has retained some 9C features: the basilica plan with a nave and two aisles, the columns with antique capitals, and the beautiful apsidal **mosaic**★. At the end of the church is an entrance to the **Villa Celimontana** park.

Basilica dei Santi Giovanni e Paolo – *Domus Antica (Ancient House): Open 8.30am–noon, 3.30–6pm.* This church was established in a private house in the 4C, and rebuilt in the 12C after being sacked by Norman troops in 1084. The Romanesque campanile rests on the foundations of the **Temple of Claudius**. The arches above the porch and the gallery belong to the original building. Beneath the church, excavations have revealed the rooms of an **ancient house**★ *(access by steps at the west end of the north aisle; 06 70 45 45 44; www.case romane.it; open Thu–Mon 10am–1pm, 3–6pm; guided tours Sat and Sun; €6)*, dating from the 2C with well-preserved pagan and Christian paintings. **Clivo di Scauro** on the left, built in 2C BC, passes under the medieval buttresses of the church.

San Gregorio Magno – *06 70 49 49 66. Open Tue–Sun 8.30am–12.30pm, 4–6.30pm. Chapels €2.60.* The imposing 17C façade of the church of St Gregory the Great is at the top of a steep flight of steps, framed by cypresses and umbrella pines. The interior is Baroque apart from the fine mosaic floor, and in the chapel at the head of the south aisle stands Gregory's Altar (15C). Another smaller chapel off this one is believed to have been Gregory's own cell, and it contains his episcopal throne. In the small square outside there are three **chapels**, linked by a portico of antique columns.

Gregory the Great (c 540–604)

Legend tells how when Pope Gregory first saw pale-skinned English slave boys in Rome he said, "They are not Angles but angels," prompting him to send St Augustine on a mission to convert England.

BATHS OF CARACALLA★★

Ⓜ *Line B: Circo Massimo*

This extensive green space centers on the enormous bathing complex where as many as 1,600 people of all social ranks could meet at the same time to bathe, exercise, and exchange gossip.

◝◞ Walking Tour

✕ **Lunch stop** – Via Guido Baccelli.

Santa Balbina – *Entrance is usually permitted from the courtyard of Santa Margherita Ospizio (Casa di Riposo), to the right of the church. 06 57 20 207. Open 9–11.30am.* This church was probably a 4C house converted into a place of worship. On the right of the entrance is Cardinal Surdi's 13C **tomb★**, bearing a recumbent Gothic figure and decorated with marble inlay. Behind the high altar is the **episcopal chair★**, a fine piece of Cosmati work (13C).

Baths of Caracalla★★ – *06 39 96 77 00. www.pierreci.it. Open daily 9am–1hr before dusk. Closed Mon afternoon, Jan 1, and Christmas. €6 (valid for 7 days for Terme di Caracalla, Villa dei Quintili, and the tomb of Cecilia Metella).* Covering 25 acres/11 ha, the baths of Emperor Antoninus Caracalla were the largest that Rome had ever seen when they were opened in AD 216. The sober exterior concealed a rich interior: marble floors, walls covered with mosaic and gilded stucco work, and white marble capitals and cornices. As well as the baths there were gymnasia,

meeting rooms, and libraries. The baths were in use until 537, when the invading Goths damaged the aqueducts that supplied Rome. In the 16C Cardinal Farnese removed a lot of the marble for his palace in the Piazza Farnese, but some of the mosaic flooring is still in place.

Santi Nereo e Achilleo – *For information on opening times, call 06 57 57 996.* A little church stood here in the 4C on the site where St Peter was supposed to have dropped a bandage that covered his wounds from the Mamertine prison chains after his escape. The church was completely rebuilt in the 9C by Leo III and restored in the 15C by Sixtus IV. In 1596 the relics of St Nereus and St Achilleus were transferred here from Domitilla's Catacombs.

San Cesareo – *To visit, contact Via di Porta S. Sebastiano 4. Donations welcome.* Little is known of this church's history before 1600, when it was restored by Cardinal Baronius. The coffered ceiling bears the arms of Clement VIII and there are paintings by Cavaliere d'Arpino. Nearby is the handsome house, **Casa del Cardinale Bessarione★**, of the 15C Humanist scholar Cardinal John Bessarion (*06 67 10 38 33; open by appointment only*).

Sepolcro degli Scipioni – *Via di Porta S. Sebastiano 9. For visitor information call 06 70 49 00 53.* The Scipio family tomb was discovered in 1780 and restored in 1926. It was built in the 3C BC for Cornelius Scipio Barbatus, and members of this military family were buried here until the middle of the 2C BC.

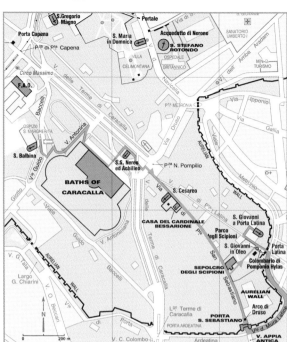

San Giovanni in Oleo – This 16C Renaissance-style octagonal temple is supposed to mark the site where St John was boiled in oil, hence its name. Nearby is the **Colombario di Pomponio Hylas** *(06 67 10 38 19; open by appointment only; €2.10)*. Decorated with stucco work and fine paintings, this cremation urn repository probably dates from the Julio–Claudian period (AD 31–68).

San Giovanni a Porta Latina – The church of St John at the Latin Gate occupies a charming **site★**; the peaceful forecourt, flanked by the campanile, has a medieval well. The **Porta Latina** in the Aurelian Wall was restored by Honorius in the 5C.

Aurelian Wall★ – Work on the this wall was initiated under Emperor Aurelian in the 3C. Most of it has survived, enclosing all of Rome's seven hills. It is a compelling piece of civil engineering, notably between the Porta Latina and **Porta San Sebastiano★**, the most spectacular in Rome, with its base of tall marble blocks supporting crenelated towers. Known as the Porta Appia in ancient times, it now houses the **Museo delle Mura** *(06 70 47 52 84; www.museo dellemuraroma.it; open Tue–Sun 9am–2pm; closed Jan 1, May 1, Christmas. €3)*, which chronicles the wall's evolution. Caracalla used the 2C **Arco di Druso** (Arch of Drusus) to support the acqueduct feeding the baths.

CENTRAL ROME

This is the Rome of *la dolce vita*, including many of it most iconic sights such as the Spanish Steps, the Trevi Fountain, and palazzo and piazza galore, along with districts full of character such as Trastevere.

QUIRINALE★★★

M *Line A: Barberini*

The Qurinal Hill is the highest of Rome's seven hills. Famous for the magnificent Trevi Fountain, the piazza has one of the best views in the city, who became chief minister of France.

●✿Walking Tour

✗ **Lunch stop** – Palazzo delle Esposizioni, Via Milano.

Fontana di Trevi★★★
see Fabulous Fountains

Santi Vincenzo e Anastasio – In front of the fountain stands the ~~Baroque~~ church dedicated to St Vincent and St Anastasius, built in 1650 for Cardinal Mazarin.

Museo Nazionale delle Paste Alimentari *see For Kids*

Piazza del Quirinale★★ – Lined with handsome palaces, this square typifies Roman elegance. The **Palazzo del Quirinale★★** *(06 46 99 1; www.quirinale.it; open Sun 8.30am–midday; closed Jan 7, Apr 8 & 29, May 27, Dec 16, 23 & 30, Jul–Sept; €5)* was commissioned in 1573 by Gregory XIII as a summer residence for the popes and is now the official residence of the President of the Republic.

Palazzo della Consulta – The Baroque **façade★** of this palace is by Ferdinando Fuga (18C). The three doorways make a lively contrast with the bare façade of the Palazzo del Quirinale.

The two churches on Via del Quirinale—**Sant'Andrea al Quirinale★★** *(06 69 70 03 06; open Wed–Mon 8.30am–noon, 4–7pm; closed Aug)* by Bernini and **San Carlo alle Quattro Fontane★★** *(open Mon–Fri 10am–1pm, 3–6pm, Sat 10am–1pm)* by Borromini—demonstrate the genius of two artists whose styles were very different.

Palazzo Pallavicini – *06 48 14 344. Open 1st of the month 10am–noon, 3–5pm (by appointment only, contact at least 3 weeks in advance). Closed Jan 1.* This palace was built by Cardinal Scipio Borghese in 1603. Inside the main gates is the **Casino★**, a 17C pavilion famous for the Aurora fresco by Guido Reni. Farther along Via 24 Maggio is the church of **San Silvestro al Quirinale** *(entrance to the left of*

Film star fountain

The Trevi Fountain featured in *Three Coins in the Fountain*, a 1950s movie about three American women looking for romance in Rome, and again in Fellini's *La Dolce Vita*, with Anita Ekberg and Marcello Mastroianni.

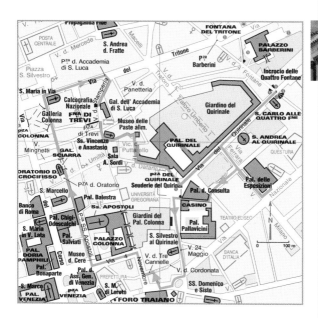

the façade, to visit ring the bell at no. 10; 06 67 90 240) whose rich interior includes a beautiful octagonal domed **chapel★**.

Galleria di Palazzo Colonna★ – 06 67 84 350. www.galleriacolonna. it. Open Sat 9am–1pm, all other days by appointment only. Closed Aug. €10. Located in the former residence of Pope Martin V, this features 15C–18C paintings, notably the famous **Peasant Eating Beans★** attributed to Annibale Carracci, and the handsome **Salone★★**. Behind the palace is the **Museo delle Cere** (see For Kids).

Basilica dei Santi Dodici Apostoli★ – 06 69 95 78 43. Open Mon–Sat 7am–noon, 4–7pm. The Basilica of the Twelve Holy Apostles dates back to the 6C. **Cardinal Pietro Riario's tomb★** is the work

of Andrea Bregno, Mino da Fiesole, and Giovanni Dalmata. The **Palazzo Chigi-Odescalchi**, in front of the basilica, was redesigned by Bernini in 1664. Opposite is the Baroque **Palazzo Balestra** where the Stuarts, the royal family of Scotland and England, recognized as the rightful kings of England by the pope, lived in exile.

The façade of the **Oratorio del Crocifisso★** (Uratory of the Crucifix) dates from 1561. The **Galleria Sciarra★** is a highly original late 19C arcade and leads on to the **Galleria Colonna** and the church of **Santa Maria in Via**.

Via del Tritone is one of the busiest shopping streets in Rome. The **Calcografia Nazionale** (6 Via della Stamperia) houses over 23,000 engravings.

PIAZZA DI SPAGNA★★★

M Line A: Spagna

The Spanish ambassador to the Holy See took up residence in the Palazzo di Spagna in the 17C, thus giving the square its name. It is one of the most popular and glamorous meeting places in the city.

✎ Walking tour

✕ **Lunch stop** – Via dei Condotti.

Fontana della Barcaccia★
see Fabulous Fountains

Scalinata della Trinità dei Monti★★★ (Spanish Steps) – Built between 1723 and 1726, the steps show the Baroque taste for *trompe l'oeil*. Three flights of steps descend gracefully and majestically. At the foot are **Casa-Museo di Giorgio de Chirico★** *(Piazza di Spagna 31; 06 67 96 546; www.fondazionedechirico.it; visits by appointment; €5)*, which displays several of his paintings including **Hector and Andromache★**, and **Casina di Keats** (Keats' House) *(Piazza di Spagna 26; 06 67 84 235; www.keats-shelley-house.org; open Mon–Fri 10am–1pm, 2–6pm, Sat 11am–2pm, 3–6pm; closed Sun, Christmas; €4)*, where the poet died in 1821.

Trinità dei Monti★ – Founded in 1495 by Charles VIII, the side chapels are decorated with Mannerist paintings, including the **Deposition from the Cross★** (1541) by Daniele da Volterra.

Villa Medici – *06 67 611. www.villamedici.it. Guided tours of the garden (advance booking required) Sat and Sun. €8.* This villa was built

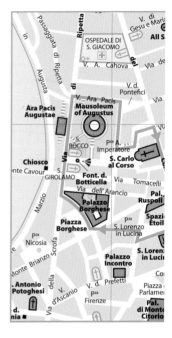

around 1570 for Cardinal Ricci di Montepulciano. The main façade contrasts sharply with the richly decorated **inner façade★**.

Returning to Trinità dei Monti and continuing along Via Gregoriana and left into Via di Capo le Case brings you to the church of **Sant'Andrea delle Fratte** with a fine **dome★** and **campanile★**. Inside are two statues of **angels★** by Bernini. Farther along Via delle Mercede is **Piazza San Silvestro**, dominated by the façade of the Central Post Office, established in the monastery of the church of **San Silvestro in Capite**. Turning right into Via del Gambero and then left into Via Frattina brings you to **Piazza San Lorenzo in Lucina** with its 12C church.

54

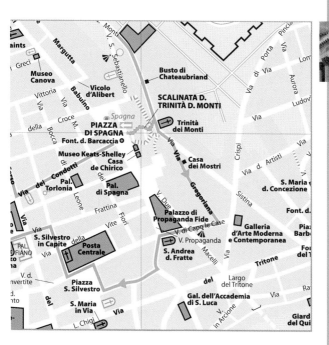

Via del Leone leads on to the late 16C **Palazzo Borghese**, which belonged to Cardinal Camillo Borghese, who became Pope Paul V in 1605. The courtyard, with its loggias, statues, and fountains, gives a glimpse into the leisured existence of Rome's noble families.

North along Via di Ripetta are the ruins of the **Mausoleum of Augustus**, one of the most sacred monuments in antiquity. A bronze statue of the emperor stood in the middle, at its highest point. The **Ara Pacis Augustae★★** (Altar of Augustus) *(06 06 08; www.arapacis. it; open Tue–Sun 9am–7pm; closed Jan 1, May 1, Christmas; €8)* is housed next to the Mausoleum in a new building, the first work of modern architecture in the historic center of Rome since the 1930s. The altar was inaugurated in 9 BC in honor of the peace that Augustus had established throughout the Roman world.

San Carlo al Corso – The **dome★** of this fine church is by Pietro da Cortona (1668). Farther along Via del Corso is the 16C **Palazzo Ruspoli**, once the glamorous artistic salon of Hortense de Beauharnais, Napoleon's stepdaughter.

Via dei Condotti is one of the most famous streets in Rome, lined with smart boutiques and elegant *palazzi* housing some of the most prestigious names in fashion. The historic **Caffé Greco**, the oldest café in Rome and a famous literary hangout, is at no. 86.

CASTEL SANT' ANGELO★★

M *Line A: Lepanto*

The old fortress looks out across the River Tiber onto the medieval commercial district, once thronged with bankers and moneylenders, now home to expensive antique shops all along Via Giulia.

🐾 Walking Tour

✖ **Lunch stop** – Restaurant in the fortress, Via Giulia.

Castel Sant' Angelo★★ – *06 681 91 11. www.castelsantangelo. com. Open Tue–Sun 9am–7pm (last admission 6.30pm). Closed Jan 1, Christmas. €5.* This papal fortress sits on a rocky outcrop and is dominated by the angel statue commemorating Gregory the Great's vision, which gave the fortress its name. Entry to the complex is through the old mausoleum entrance.

The **Mausoleo di Adriano** was begun by Emperor Hadrian in AD 135 as a sepulcher for himself and his family. The mausoleum contained the urns of all the emperors from Hadrian to Septimius Severus. The mausoleum was incorporated into Aurelian's fortifications around the city in 270. During the medieval struggle between the papacy and the noble families, the structure became a papal stronghold. A brick story was added on top of the mausoleum and the octagonal bastions were the work of Alexander VI. During the 16C improvements were made to the living quarters and the ramparts around the fortress were added in the 17C. After unification, Castel Sant'Angelo became a barracks and military prison.

A high defensive wall – the **Passetto** – built by Leo IV (847–55) links the castle to the Vatican Palace. Alexander VI built a passage along the top, so the pope could retreat if there was a siege.

A **spiral ramp** leads up to the chamber where the funeral urns were kept when the castle was a mausoleum. The walls were originally covered in marble and the floor was paved with mosaic.

On the right of the **main courtyard** are medieval rooms, now the lower armoury. The end of the courtyard is closed by a shrine designed by Michelangelo. On the left of the courtyard are the papal rooms, the **Sala dell'Apollo** and the **Sala di Clemente VII**. The Sala dell'Apollo takes its name from its paintings of mythological figures. The wooden ceilings of the Sala di Clemente VII bear the pope's name and are decorated with 15C and 16C paintings.

The beautiful decor of the **Bagno di Clemente VII★** by Giovanni da Udine, a pupil of Raphael, reveals the civilized lifestyle of the 16C popes. By contrast the dank **prison** is supposed to have held Giordano Bruno, the heretic monk, and the sculptor Benvenuto Cellini.

The **oil and grain store** was provisioned by Alexander VI in case of siege. The jars could hold 4,839gal/22,000l of oil and the capacity of the five large silos was about 3,700cwt/100kg of grain.

MUST SEE

The steps up from Alexander VI's court lead to the **Loggia di Pio IV**, the **Loggia di Paolo III**, and the **Loggia di Giulio II**. The rooms that open onto Pius IV's loggia were living quarters for the staff. In the 19C the loggia was rebuilt to house political prisoners. Pope Paul III commissioned Antonio da Sangallo (the Younger) to design a loggia in 1543 and had it decorated with stucco work and grotesques. Past the restaurant and the upper armory, which contains arms and uniforms of the Italian and papal armies, is Julius II's loggia. This faces south with a fine view of Ponte Sant'Angelo and the city. It was probably designed by Giuliano da Sangallo.

The **papal apartment★** was built after the siege of 1527. These rooms are protected by a succession of ramps and steps. The **Sala del Consiglio** or **Sala Paolina** was a waiting room for visitors to the pope. Its floor is marble and the frescoes are by a group of artists instructed by Perin del Vagal. The **Camera del Perseo** takes its name from the frieze by del Vaga. In the **Camera di Amore e Psiche**, the frieze illustrates the story of the beautiful girl beloved by Venus's son.

From the Sala del Consiglio a corridor leads up to the **library** and then to **Hadrian's Mausoleum Room** and the **Festoon Room**. The **Sala del Tesoro**, at the center of the fortress, is a circular chamber that holds the papal records, transferred here from the Vatican in 1870. Beside the Sala del Tesoro the **Scala Romana** leads to the **Hall of Flags and Columns** (Sala Rotonda) and the **terrace**. From here you can survey a magnificent **panorama★★★** of the city, extending from the Prati district and the Villa Borghese on the left, past the Quirinal Palace and the shallow dome of the Pantheon, to St Peter's and the Vatican. You can also walk along the parapets to the corner bastions, each named after one of the Evangelists.

Palazzo di Giustizia – Along from the Castel Sant'Angelo, the Law Courts, built between 1889 and 1911 by Guglielmo Calderini are among the most conspicuous modern buildings in Rome.

D. Chapuis/MICHELIN

Castel Sant'Angelo

Ponte Sant'Angelo★ – This elegant bridge dates back to Hadrian's era, though it was altered significantly when the Tiber embankments were built in 1892–94. The ten Baroque angels are the work of Bernini. Across the bridge at the end of Via Paola is the church of **San Giovanni dei Fiorentini** *(open 9am–noon, 3–6pm)*, built by the Florentine Pope Leo X. Its eclectic styling includes a Baroque chancel and an 18C façade. Borromini's tomb is near the main altar.

Via Giulia★ – Part of the pilgrimage route, this wide avenue once led the faithful to St Peter's. Goldsmith Benvenuto Cellini lived here, as did Sangallo the Younger and Raphael. At no. 66 is the **Palazzo Sacchetti**, which may have been designed by Sangallo the Younger, architect of the Farnese Palace. No. 52 houses the **Museum of Criminology** *(entrance on Via del Gonfalone 29; 06 68 89 94 42; www.museocriminologico.it; open Tue–Sat 9am–1pm, Tue & Thu 2.30–6.30pm; closed Mon, Sun, public holidays and Aug 13–25; €2)*, which was once a model prison built by Pope Innocent X.

Turning left into Vicolo del Malpasso and left again into Via dei Banchi Vecchi brings you to the **Palazzo Sforza Cesarini**, built by Pope Alexander VI, when he was a mere cardinal. On the other side of Corso Vittorio Emanuele II is the **Chiesa Nuova**★ (New Church) *(open 8am–noon, 4.30–7pm)*. Founded in the 12C as Santa Maria in Vallicella the church was rebuilt in 1605 as the New Church by St Philip Neri, the Florentine founder of the Oratorians. The interior has an elaborate Baroque format inspired by Pietro da Cortona, who painted *St Philip's Vision* (1664–65) on the stucco ceiling. St Philip's remains are in the grandiose chapel. There are a number of Mannerist and Baroque paintings here, including three early works by Rubens. Next to the church is the **Oratorio dei Filippini**, built between 1637 and 1662 to house the assemblies of the Oratorians.Now known as Borromini Hall, it hosts conferences and various cultural activities and houses the archives of the city of Rome. The **façade**★ overlooking Piazza della Chiesa Nuova was designed by Borromini to form a unit with the church. In front of the church is the **Fontana della "Terrina,"** carved in 1590.

Turn right from the church into **Via del Governo Vecchio**, one of the district's main streets, lined with artisans' workshops, junk shops, and antique dealers. At no. 39 is the **Palazzo del Governo Vecchio**, the residence of the Governor of Rome in the 17C. By Piazza di Pasquino sits the **Pasquino**, a statuary group where citizens have posted anti-government rants since the 16C. Turning back, you come to the **Piazza dell'Orologio** with its graceful clock tower.

Benvenuto Cellini (1500–1571)
Talented artist and goldsmith, Cellini was a larger than life character who recounted his exploits, including murder, unashamedly in a famous racy autobiography.

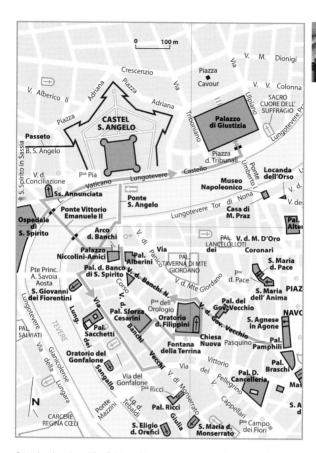

Straight ahead are **Via dei Banchi Nuovi** and **Via Banco di Santo Spirito**, where moneylenders from Florence, Siena, and Genoa were active in the 15C. They were closely linked to the Holy See, which granted them concessions on mining and customs dues. Until 1541, a mint inhabited the **Palazzo del Banco di Santo Spirito**.

To the right is **Via dei Coronari★**, one of the city's most attractive streets, with antique shops and red stone palaces. On the left is the **Arco dei Banchi** (Bankers' Arch) leading on to the **Ponte Vittorio Emanuele II**. This was begun soon after Italian unification and completed in 1911. Across the bridge on the left is the imposing **Santo Spirito Hospital**, and beyond the 16C church of **Santo Spirito in Sassia** (open 9am–7pm) by Sangallo the Younger. To the right is the little church of the **Santissima Annunciata**, with its attractive 18C façade.

MONTECITORIO★★

Ⓜ *Line A: Spagna*

This district was extensively restored by the Renaissance popes, and the narrow streets around the square are full of luxury stores, while farther afield there are arts and crafts workshops.

🐟 Walking Tour

✕ **Lunch stop** – Piazza di Montecitorio.

Piazza di Montecitorio – This square features an **Egyptian obelisk**, brought back from Heliopolis by Augustus in 10 BC. It was the pointer for a gigantic sundial. On the north side of square is the **Palazzo di Montecitorio** *(06 67 601; guided tour of the Chamber of Deputies 1st Sun of the month 10am–6pm; times may vary, check www.camera.it, in "Servizi ai Cittadini"; closed Aug–Sept)*. This has been the seat of Italy's Chamber of Deputies since 1870, and was begun in 1650 by Bernini and

completed 47 years later by Carlo Fontana. Little remains of Bernini's Baroque fantasies: rough-hewn stones frame some windows and the effect is quite rustic.

Piazza Colonna★ – This is one of the most crowded squares in Rome, sitting at the junction of the two main shopping streets, Via del Corso and Via del Tritone. The **column★** in the middle was was erected in honor of Marcus Aurelius and has reliefs showing significant episodes from his wars. In 1589, Pope Sixtus V replaced the statue of the emperor on top of the column with one of St Paul. On the north side of the square is the **Palazzo Chigi**, built between 1562 and 1630. Two decades later, Pope Alexander VII purchased it for his family, after whom it is named. Taking the street between Palazzo di Montecitorio and Palazzo Chigi and following the road left and left again brings you to Via di Campo Marzio, which was once occupied by a huge **solar clock** built by Augustus.

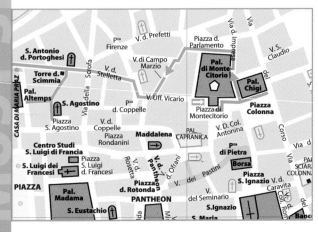

Monkey business

According to legend, the family who lived in the Torre della Scimmia owned a monkey (*scimmia* in Italian) that stole a newborn child and climbed to the top of the tower with the baby in its paws. The terrified father prayed to the Virgin and the baby was returned safe and sound. In gratitude, a shrine to the Virgin was erected, in front of which a light has been kept burning ever since.

Sant'Antonio dei Portoghesi – *06 68 80 24 96. Open daily 8.30am–1pm, 3–6pm. The church is also open periodically for classical music concerts and recitals.* The 17C Portuguese national church has a Rococo façade and the interior is richly decorated with gold, stucco, marble, and paintings. The first chapel on the right contains a monument by Canova.

Torre della Scimmia – The building on the corner of Via dei Portoghesi and Via dei Pianellari has a 15C tower known as the Monkey Tower.

Sant'Agostino★ – *06 60 80 19 62. Open Mon–Sat 7am–1pm, 4.30–7pm, Sun 3.30–7pm.* This church, dedicated to St Augustine of Hippo, was built between 1479 and 1483. The broad travertine façade, with its rose windows, is a fine example of Renaissance style. Inside there are several important works of art: near the main door is the **Madonna del Parto★** (1521) by Jacopo Sansovino. The third pillar on the left in the nave bears a fresco by Raphael (1512) of the **Prophet Isaiah★**. The first chapel on the left contains the **Madonna of the Pilgrims★★★** (1605) by Caravaggio, which was criticized by contemporaries for showing ugly, ordinary people instead of idealized pilgrims.

Palazzo Altemps★★★ – *see Major Museums*

Returning to San Antonio dei Portoghesi and walking west along Via dell'Orso brings you to **Locanda dell'Orso** (Bear Inn). From the Middle Ages to the Renaissance this district was full of inns, providing lodgings for pilgrims on their way to St Peter's. French essayist Michel de Montaigne stayed in this 15C inn for a few days during his visit to Rome in 1580.

At the end of Via dell'Orso in Piazza di Ponte Umberto I are two museums. The **Museo Napoleonico★** (*06 68 80 62 86; www.museonapoleonico.it; open Tue–Sun 9am–7pm; closed Jan 1, May 1 and Christmas; €3*) was founded in 1927 by Giuseppe Primoli, a descendant of Lucien Bonaparte, and contains souvenirs of the Napoleonic presence in the city. Next door is the **Casa di Mario Praz** (*06 68 61 089; www. museopraz.beniculturali.it; open Tue–Sun 9am–2pm, 2.30–7.30pm; guided tours only, 45min; closed Jan 1, Christmas*). This was the house of the literary critic Mario Praz (d. 1982). He accumulated a huge amount of Neoclassical furniture and *objets d'art*, including a rare collection of 17C–19C wax models.

PIAZZA NAVONA★★★

Ⓜ *Line A: Spagna*

The stadium built by Domitian for athletics and poetry competitions has given this square its long narrow shape. Today, set apart from the thrum of traffic, it seems to be on permanent holiday.

🐌Walking Tour

✕ **Lunch stop** – Piazza Navona, Via della Pace, Piazza Sant'Eustachio.

Piazza Navona★★★ – Domitian's stadium was in ruins by the 5C, but the site was revived by the Renaissance popes and features buildings by some of the most famous architects of the 16C and 17C, notably Bernini, who was responsible for the **Fontana dei Fiumi★★★** *(see Fabulous Fountains)*. On the west side of the square is the church of **Sant'Agnese in Agone★★** *(06 68 19 21 34; open Tue–Sun 9.30am–12.30pm, 4–7pm)*. In 1652, Pope Innocent X commissioned this church as a family chapel attached to his palace, the **Palazzo Pamphili**. The rich decoration of the **interior★** dates from the end of the 17C.

Leaving the square at the north end you can see the remains of **Domitian's Stadium** in Via di Tor Sanguigna. On Via della Pace is the entrance to the church of **Santa Maria dell'Anima** *(open daily 9.30am–1pm, 3–7pm)*. This is the church of German-speaking Roman Catholics and the present building was begun in 1500. The Renaissance **façade** in Via dell'Anima was designed by Giuliano da Sangallo and built in 1511.

From piazza to pool
In the 17 and 18C the piazza was sometimes flooded in the summer and turned into a lake for aquatic games or reconstructions of naval battles, often masterminded by the powerful Pamphili family.

Santa Maria della Pace★ – *06 68 61 156. Open 10am–12.30pm, 4–6pm. Closed Sun afternoon, public holidays.* The original 12C church was rebuilt by Sixtus IV in 1480, and Pietro da Cortona designed a new **façade** in the mid-17C. The first chapel on the right has a painting of the four **Sibyls★** by Raphael. The first chapel on the left has frescoes by Baldassare Peruzzi. The handsome **cloisters** house a pretty café.

Heading south and then left into Via del Governo Vecchio brings you to the **Palazzo Braschi★** of Pope Pius VI, the last papal family palace erected in Rome. It houses the **Museo di Roma★** *(06 67 10 83 46; http://en.museodiroma.it; open Tue–Sun 9am–7pm (Dec 24 & 31 2pm); closed Jan 1, May 1, Christmas; €8)*, whose paintings and **frescoes★** trace the history of the city from the Middle Ages to the present. On the second floor are the famous **watercolors★** in the series "Lost Rome" *(Roma sparita)*. A little farther along, next door to the church of **San Pantaleo**, is the **Palazzo Massimo**, which belongs to one of the oldest families in Rome. The façade facing onto Corso Vittorio Emanuele II features a fine curved portico of Doric columns by Baldassare Peruzzi.

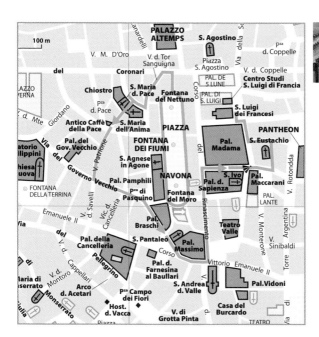

Palazzo della Sapienza –
This palazzo was the seat of the
University of Rome from the
15C until 1935. At the end of the
inner courtyard is the church of
Sant'Ivo alla Sapienza★★ *(06 68
64 987; open Mon–Fri 10am–4pm,
Sat 10am–1pm, Sun 9am–noon)*.
The striking façade is by Borromini.
From Piazza Sant'Eustachio there
is a splendid **view★★** of its spiral
dome. On the south side stands
the **Palazzo Maccarani**, an austere building in the Renaissance
style with a popular café, and the
church of **Sant'Eustachio**.

San Luigi dei Francesi★★ –
*06 68 82 71. Open 8.30am–12.30pm,
3.30–7.30pm. Closed Thu afternoons.*
This 16C church was consecrated
as the national church of the
French in Rome. The **façade** was
probably designed by Giacomo
della Porta. Inside is the beautiful
chapel of St Cecilia with **frescoes
by Domenichino★** and the
chapel of St Matthew with three
magnificent **frescoes by Cara-
vaggio★★★**. Next door is the 16C
Medici **Palazzo Madama** *(closed
to the public)*, which houses the
Senate of the Italian Republic.

Fontana del Fiumi

In 1651, in order to finance the spiraling costs of Bernini's spectacular
fountain, special taxes were raised, including one on bread. We may
appreciate the result now but it was not a popular move at the time!

CENTRAL ROME

PIAZZA DELLA ROTONDA

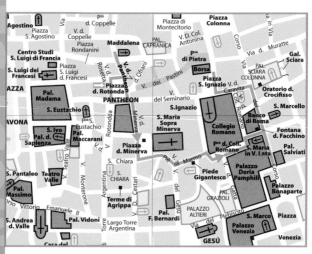

Ⓜ *Line A: Spagna*

This square is on part of the Campus Martius, a marshy plain used by the ancient Romans for drilling soldiers. Dominated by the magnificent Pantheon, the square has several fine Classical and Baroque buildings.

✿▸Walking Tour

✕ **Lunch stop** – Via degli Orfani.

Piazza della Rotonda – At the center of the square is a fountain designed in 1578 by Giacomo Della Porta, and at no. 63 on the east side is the 15C **Albergo del Sole** (Hotel of the Sun) one of the oldest inns in the city. To the north is Piazza della Maddalena and the church of **Santa Maria Maddalena** *(06 67 97 796; open Mon–Fri 6am–7pm, Sat–Sun and public holidays, 9am–7pm)*, which stands

on the site of a 15C hospice. The relics of St Camillus of Lellis, who founded a nursing order that ran the hospice, are venerated at the altar in the south transept. The church was rebuilt in the 17C by Carlo Fontana, and the **interior★** is a rare example of the Rococo in Rome.

Piazza della Minerva – This square to the south of the **Pantheon★★★** *(see Major Churches)* features an Egyptian obelisk supported on a marble elephant sculpted by one of Bernini's pupils, Ercole Ferrata. The church of **Santa Maria sopra Minerva★★** *(06 67 93 926; www.basilicaminerva. it; open daily 9am–7pm; cloister: 8am–1pm, 3.30–7.30pm)* is Rome's only Gothic church. Dating from the 13C, its name "Saint Mary over Minerva," refers to the ruins of a temple to the Roman goddess nearby. The church has long been the headquarters of the Dominicans. It houses a number of important **works of art★** including a statue of the **Risen Christ★** by Michelangelo to the left of the high altar. The Carafa Chapel is decorated with **frescoes★** by Filippino Lippi. **St Catherine of Siena's Chapel** was built using the walls of the room from the convent where the saint died. Her tomb is under the main altar, and other notable tombs include those of Cardinal Coca decorated by Andrea Bregno, Fra Angelico in the north transept, and the funeral monuments of the Medici Popes, Clement VII, and Leo V.

Walking east along Via Piè di Marmo, named after a huge **stone foot** that stands here, brings you to the Piazza del Collegio Romano. The **Collegio Romano** was founded in 1583 by Gregory XIII, who strove to re-establish the primacy of Rome after the Council of Trent.

Palazzo Doria Pamphili★ – One of Rome's largest palaces, this was begun in the 15C and gradually enlarged by a succession of noble owners. The façade facing Via del Corso is an imposing 18C construction in the Baroque style, whereas the front onto Via del Plebiscito dates from 1643. The palace houses a fine **gallery★★** (see Major Museums) and since the official visit of the Archbishop of Canterbury in 1966 it has also been the Anglican Centre in Rome. South along Via del Corso is the church of **Santa Maria in Via Lata** with its columned Baroque façade by Pietro Cortona. Farther along is the 17C **Palazzo Salviati**, built by the Duke of Nevers to house the French Academy.

G. Bludzin/MICHELIN

Detail of Annunciation by FilippinoLippi in the Carafa Chapel, Santa Maria sopra Minerva

San Marcello – *Open daily 7.45am (Sun 9.30am)–noon, 4–7pm.* Opposite the 18C **Palazzo del Banco di Roma** is the church of St Marcellus, founded in the 4C on the site of a private house used for Christian worship. After a fire in 1519 it was completely rebuilt in the 16C and 17C. The 16C nave with side chapels, typical of the Renaissance, was designed by Jacopo Sansovino. In the fourth chapel on the right is a fine 15C wooden crucifix.

Piazza Sant'Ignazio★ – To the north of the Collegio Romano this charming square has curved façades on the street corners. The 1626 church of **Sant'Ignazio★★** *(open daily 7.30am–12.30pm, 3–7pm)* is dedicated to the founder of the Jesuit Order. The stunning central vault **fresco★★** and the *trompe-l'œil* cupola are best viewed from the disk in the center of the nave. The fresco is the work of Andrea Pozzo, a Jesuit, and shows St Ignatius bathed by a divine light. To the north of Piazza Sant'Ignazio is **Piazza di Pietra** whose south side is occupied by the Stock Exchange.

CAMPO DEI FIORI★★

Ⓜ Line A: Spagna

The "Field of Flowers" was a vast meadow in the Middle Ages, and was the venue for all sorts of festivals. The square hosts an early morning food market and is bustling from then until after midnight.

✎ Walking Tour

✕ **Lunch stop** – Café on the square.

Piazza Campo dei Fiori★ – In the 16C Rome's center was a meeting place for people of all ranks. The **"Hostaria della Vacca"** belonged to Vanozza Caetani, famous for her liaison with Rodrigo Borgia, later Pope Alexander VI.

Palazzo della Cancelleria★★ – *06 98 87 556/617. Visits by appointment only. Apply to the Papal Commission at Palazzo della Cancelleria, Piazza della Cancelleria 1.* The Chancery Palace was built between 1483 and 1513 for Cardinal Raffaele Riario, and now houses the Papal Chancery. This *palazzo* is the most elegant product of Rome's Renaissance. Within the palace is the church of **San Lorenzo in Damaso**, founded by Pope Damasus in the 4C.

Palazzo della Farnesina ai Baullari★ – This Renaissance building was begun in 1523 for Thomas le Roy, a French diplomat. It houses a fine collection of ancient sculpture left by Baron Giovanni Barracco *(06 68 80 68 48 or 06 82 05 91 27; www.museo barracco.it; open Tue–Sun 9am–*

7pm; closed Jan 1, May 1, Christmas; €3). Farther along is **Piazza Sant'Andrea della Valle**, with a fountain attributed to Carlo Maderno.

Sant'Andrea della Valle★★ – This church was begun in 1591 under the direction of Giacomo della Porta and completed between 1608 and 1623 by Maderno. The elegant Baroque **façade★★** was built by Carlo Rainaldi. The **dome★★** is one of the loveliest in the city and second only to St Peter's in size. The upper section of the **apse★** dates from the late Renaissance.

Cappella del Monte di Pietà★ – *06 67 07 84 95. Open mornings by appointment only.* This gem of Baroque art was originally the work of Carlo Maderno.

Palazzo Spada★ – *06 68 32 409. The Piano Nobile is open on the 1st Sun of the month only, in the morning.* Cardinal Gerolamo Capo di Ferro built this lavish white stucco edifice, later acquired by Cardinal Bernardino Spada. The palace houses the **Galleria Spada★** *(06 68 32 409; www.galleriaborghese. it; open Tue–Sun 8.30am–7.30pm; closed Jan 1, May 1, Christmas; €5),* which presents the Cardinal's collection in its original setting, featuring works by Guercino, Guido Reni, Bruegel the Elder, Pietro Testa, and Artemisia Gentileschi. The delicate friezes in the **courtyard★★** are enchanting and on the ground floor is a Borromini "Perspective" *(inquire about access),* a colonnade that appears to stretch into the distance, though it is only 9m/29ft long.

Palazzo Farnese★★ – *06 68 89 28 18. www.ambafrance-it.org. Guided tours only (50min), Mon & Thu at 3pm, 4pm, 5pm.* One of the most beautiful Roman palaces, this carries the family name of Pope Paul III, who commissioned it in 1515 while still a cardinal, to designs by Antonio da Sangallo the Younger. The **façade** is a masterpiece of balance and proportion. Michelangelo was responsible for the impressive upper cornice and the central balcony. The rear **façade**—overlooking Via Giulia—by Vignola is the building's most elegant feature. Its treasures include frescoes by Annibale Carracci. The "Passetto Farnese," the graceful archway over Via Giulia by Michelangelo, was the first part of an unrealized scheme to link the palace with the Villa Farnesina on the other side of the river. **Santa Maria dell'Orazione e della Morte** was dedicated to the burial of the poor, and the façade reflects this mission: gaping skulls flank the door.

Sant'Eligio degli Orefici – *06 68 68 260. To visit, press the intercom at Via S. Eligio 9 (custodian) or Via S. Eligio 7 (office). Donations welcome. Open 10–11am. Closed July 28, Sept 3, Dec 22–31.* Raphael began this church dedicated to St Eligus, the patron saint of goldsmiths, often considered one of the purest expressions of the Renaissance. On Via di Monserrato is the charming **Palazzo Ricci**, tucked in at the back of its attractive little Renaissance square. Via di Monserrato is also the location of **Santa Maria di Monserrato**, the Spanish national church.

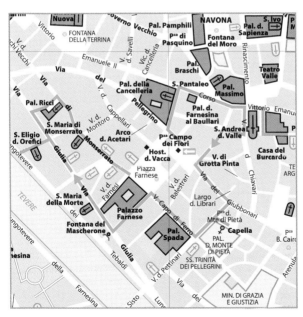

PIAZZA VENEZIA★

Ⓜ *Line B: Colosseo*

The overbearing monument to Victor Emmanuel II completed in 1911 dominates this square, which is a convenient meeting point as it is at the hub of the city's principal thoroughfares.

🐾 Walking Tour

✕ **Lunch stop** – Piazza Venezia.

Piazza Venezia★ – This grand Renaissance square used to be much more compact, with the south side being closed by the Palazzetto Venezia, the smaller counterpart to the more famous Palazzo Venezia. When the palazzetto was "moved" to its present position at the far end of Piazza San Marco it spoiled the subtle balance of the square.

Monumento a Vittorio Emanuele II (Vittoriano) – *06 69 91 718. Open 9am–5.30pm (winter 4.30pm). Closed Christmas, Jan 1.* This huge monument by

Giuseppe Sacconi honors King Victor Emmanuel II, who presided over the unification of Italy in 1870. The dazzling white marble clashes with the warm tones of the cityscape and the pompous style has led to many insulting nicknames, including "the wedding cake" and "typewriter." A flight of steps leads up to the **Altare della Patria** (Altar to the Nation) where an eternal flame burns before the tomb of the unknown soldier.

Palazzo Venezia★ – This is one of the city's most prestigious buildings. It was begun in 1455 by Cardinal Pietro Barbo and was later altered several times. The crenelations on the façade overlooking Piazza Venezia reflect the style of the fortified houses of the Middle Ages. The courtyard has a flourishing garden, flanked on two sides by an elegant portico by Giuliano da Maiano. The attractive fountain dates from the 18C. The *palazzetto* that stood at the foot of the tower was pulled down and put up again in its present position in 1910 when the square was laid out in

Monumento a Vittorio Emanuele II

©Luis Pedrosa/iStockphoto.com

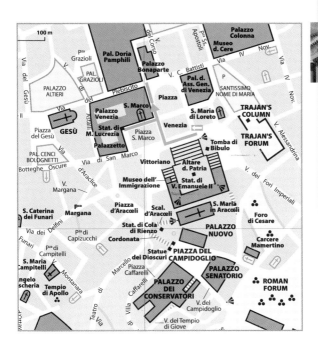

front of the monument. At the same time the **Palazzo delle Assicurazioni Generali di Venezia** was built on the other side of the square as a counterpoint to the larger Palazzo Venezia.

The museum on the first floor *(06 69 99 43 18. www.galleriaborghese. it; open Tue–Sun 8.30am–7.30pm; closed Jan 1, May 1, Christmas; €4)* is notable for its collection of medieval art, including some interesting antique ceramics. Highlights are the fine Byzantine enamel **Christ Pantocrator★★** from the second half of the 13C, a very finely carved ivory **Byzantine Triptych★★** from the 10C, and a collection of paintings on wood by primitive artists from Florence and Siena belonging to the **Sterbini Collection★★**.

Basilica di San Marco – Founded in 336, this basilica was rebuilt by Gregory IV in the 9C. In 1455 it was rebuilt again and incorporated into the Palazzo Venezia by Cardinal Pietro Barbo. The Renaissance **façade★** overlooking Piazza San Marco is particularly elegant. The sumptuous **interior★** has overlapping styles, the medieval basilica plan of a nave, and two aisles that contrast with the elegant 15C coffered ceiling.

Palazzo Bonaparte – This 17C palace was once the property of Napoleon's mother, who lived here from the fall of the empire until her death in 1836.

Chiesa del Gesù★★★ – see *Major Churches*

ISOLA TIBERINA★★

Ⓜ *Line B: Circo Massimo*

Tiber Island is a peaceful haven, contrasting with the bustle of the old Jewish quarter. The area from here toward the Piazza della Bocca della Verità is peppered with remains of ancient temples and monuments.

➸ Walking Tour

✕ **Lunch stop** – Via delle Zoccolette, Via del Portico d'Ottavia

Isola Tiberina★ – Legend links this boat-shaped island to Aesculapius, the god of medicine. The Romans built a temple on the spot where he is supposed to have landed in 293 BC. The sanctuary site is now occupied by the church of **San Bartolomeo** whose Baroque façade and 12C Romanesque bell-tower rise from the center of the island. The Hospital of the Brothers of St John of God continues the island's historical medical tradition.

Ponte Rotto – The "Broken Bridge" is what remains of the Pons Aemilius, built in the mid-2C BC. The 1C **Ponte Cestio** (Pons Cestius) links Tiber Island to bustling Trastevere. It was partially rebuilt in the 19C. On the north side of the island **Ponte Fabricio★** (Pons Fabricius), built in 62 BC, is the only intact Classical span in Rome.

The Jewish Ghetto – There has been a Jewish presence in Rome since ancient times, first in Trastevere, then from the 13C on the left bank of the Tiber. In 1556, Pope Paul IV had this area enclosed within a wall, which ran from Ponte Fabricio, along Via del Portico d'Ottavia and around Piazza delle Cinque Scole. This disease-ridden ghetto was home to some 4,000 people and was locked from dusk to dawn. In 1885 the district was completely demolished, with the exception of the houses on Via della Reginella. In 1943 more than 3,000 ghetto residents were deported; few returned. Today the district has a lively atmosphere. The **synagogue**, inaugurated in 1904, is dominated by its large dome, visible from all over Rome. Inside is the **Museo della Comunità Ebraica** *(06 68 40 06 61; www.museoebraico.roma.it; open mid-Jun–Sept Sun–Thu 10am–6.15pm, Fri 10am–3.15pm, Sept–mid-Jun, Sun–Thu 10am–4.15pm, Fri 9am–1.15pm, closed Sat, Jewish holidays; guided tours available; €7.50)*, a display of artifacts of the Jewish community in Rome, together with liturgical articles.

Piazza della Bocca della Verità★ – This square to the south of the Jewish Ghetto more or less covers the site of the **Forum Boarium**, the ancient cattle market that extended to the foot of the Aventine and reached as far east as the Arco di Giano. The remains of numerous ancient temples and sanctuaries were uncovered in this area during the 1930s. The square takes its name from a marble disk, the "Mouth of Truth," in the porch of **⛪ Santa Maria in Cosmedin★★** *(see Major Churches)*, which is supposed to bite the hand of anyone with a guilty conscience. The **Tempio della Fortuna Virile★**, one of the best-preserved temples in Rome, is probably a sanctuary to Portumnus, the god of rivers and harbors. The **Tempio di Vesta★** was actually sacred to Hercules, as shown by the base of the statue of the god found nearby. This elegant building dates from the reign of Augustus.

The 4C **Arco di Giano** has four arches and spanned a busy crossroads. It is named after Janus, who had the power to protect junctions. The **Arco degli Argentari** is a monumental gate next to San Giorgio in Velabro. The Guild of Moneychangers built it to honor Emperor Septimius Severus and his wife, Giulia Domna, who both appear on the arch.

San Giorgio in Velabro★ – Founded in the 7C, the church was rebuilt and enlarged by Pope Gregory IV. Since its 1926 restoration, San Giorgio in Velabro has recaptured the charm of the Roman churches of the Middle Ages. The façade, the porch, and the belltower are 12C.

Oratorio di San Giovanni Decollato★ – *Visit by guided tour by appointment only. Apply to Governatore della Circonfraternità della Misericordia, Via San Giovanni Decollato 22, 00186 Roma. 06 67 91 890 (mornings only).* The Oratory of the Confraternity of St John the Beheaded was built at the end of

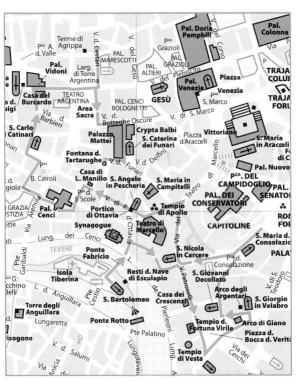

The Cenci scandal

Francesco Cenci was a cruel man who abused his children and was alleged to have committed incest with his daughter Beatrice. In spite of their complaints the authorities did nothing, and eventually Beatrice conspired with her brothers to murder their father. There was a public outcry, but Pope Clement VIII sentenced them to death and they were beheaded on September 11, 1599.

the 15C to assist people who had been condemned to death. The decoration is by a group of Mannerist artists drawing inspiration from Michelangelo and Raphael. Continuing to the north and east brings you to the church of **Santa Maria della Consolazione** *(open 7am–noon, 3.30–6pm)*. The first church was built in 1470. In the 16C a hospital was added, according to plans by Martino Longhi the Elder. He also began the façade of the church, which was eventually completed in the 19C.

Returning back down Vico Jugario brings you to the little 11C church of **San Nicola in Carcere** *(06 68 89 27 81; open daily 9am–7pm; closed Aug, Christmas)*, which stands on the ruins of three Republican temples that overlooked the Forum Holitorium, the vegetable market that extended from the Portico di Ottavia along the riverbank to Vicus Jugarius. The words *"in carcere"* refer to a Byzantine prison that occupied one of the temples.

Portico di Ottavia – Augustus rebuilt this portico and dedicated it to his sister Octavia. All that remains is part of the entrance porch *(propylaea)*. The lower archeological area is accessible via a pedestrian passage *(open 9am–dusk)*. The *propylaea* serves

as a monumental entrance to the little church of **Sant'Angelo in Pescheria**, founded in the 8C. The name recalls the fish market that occupied the antique ruins in the 12C. To the left is **Piazza delle Cinque Scole** and the **Palazzo Cenci** whose owners were involved in a famous 16C scandal. The palace is built on the rubble from some ancient buildings, perhaps the Circus Flaminius.

San Carlo ai Catinari – *Open 9am–noon, 4–6pm.* The grandiose Counter-Reformation façade of this church in Via dei Giubbonari was erected between 1635 and 1638. The **interior★** is dominated by a handsome coffered dome. Domenichino painted the Cardinal Virtues on the pendentives of the dome and in the apse is the *Apotheosis of St Charles Borromeo* by Lanfranco.

Casa del Burcardo – *06 68 19 471. www.burcardo.org. Open Mon–Fri 9am–1.30pm. Closed public holidays, Aug.* Johannes Burckard, the papal Master of Ceremonies, built this house in Via Sudario in 1503. The house is in the Gothic and Renaissance style and contains a library and a collection of theatrical costumes, masks, and playbills. At nos. 10–16 is the **Palazzo Vidoni**, designed in 1500 by Raphael for the Caffarelli, a rich Roman family. Farther along is the **Teatro Argentina**, scene of one of the most resounding failures in the annals of opera, the first performance of Rossini's *Barber of Seville* in 1816.

Area Sacra del Largo Argentina★★ – The Largo Argentina Sacred Precincts is a group of Roman Republican ruins. Traces of five levels from the 5C BC to the beginning of the Empire have been revealed. Archeologists have not established which deities were honored here, so the temples are known as A, B, C, and D.
Temple C, the oldest, dates back to the 6C or 5C BC and follows the Etruscan model: a triple *cella* with three shrines and a high podium without columns.
Temple A dates from the 4C or 3C BC. The present remains are from the 2C or 1C BC. Temple A was converted into a church to St Nicholas. The 2C BC circular **Temple B** may have been dedicated to Juno. The tufa podium was covered by one of peperine, smothered in turn by stucco. Most of **Temple D** lies beneath the Via Florida. The north and east sides of the precinct were bounded by a portico (1). The high wall (2) on the west side behind Temple A belonged to a public lavatory. Farther south, several large blocks (3) have been identified as the remains of Pompey's Curia, where Julius Caesar was assassinated in 44 BC.

Following Via de' Cestari and turning left into Via Arco della Ciambella brings you to a small fragment of wall wedged between nos. 9 and 15. This is all that remains of the **Terme di Agrippa**, the oldest baths in Rome. Built in 19 BC, these were supplied by a purpose-built aqueduct. Returning south brings you to **Via delle Botteghe Oscure**, famous in the Middle Ages for its dimly lit basement shops, which were set up in the ruins of the theater of Lucius Cornelius Balbus (1C BC). The **Crypta Balbi** *(06 39 96 77 00; www.pierreci.it; open Tue–Sun 9am–7.45pm; closed Jan 1, Christmas; €7)*, part of the Museo Nazionale Romano, is housed in medieval buildings above a portico that was added to the theater in 13 BC. The displays explain the history of the site through archeological finds.

Via Caetani contains the **Palazzo Mattei**, built by Carlo Maderno in the 17C, and the 16C church of **Santa Caterina dei Funari** with its graceful façade and unusual belltower. Around the corner is the **Fontana delle Tartarughe★** *(see Fabulous Fountains)*.

AREA SACRA DEL LARGO ARGENTINA
0   30 m
— The remains of St. Nicholas church
▬ Parts remaining   Parts no longer remaining

TRASTEVERE★★

The inhabitants of this vibrant district, whose name derives from "across the Tiber," have a certain roguish independence and a keen sense of identity, celebrated each July by the traditional "Festa de'Noantri." To the northwest is the Gianicolo, a cool leafy hill with superb views of the city.

༻🐟 Walking Tour

✖ **Lunch stop** – Via G.C. Santini, Via di S. Dorotea, Piazza Trilussa.

San Crisogono – This 12C church was extensively refurbished in the 17C. The **façade** is the work of Giovanni Battista Soria, who also redesigned the **interior★** with its large windows and fine coffered ceiling. Below floor level archeologists have discovered traces of the 5C **Palaeo Christian church** *(access from the sacristy by an awkward iron stair; 06 58 18 225; open Mon–Sat 7.30–11.15am, 4.30–7pm, Sun and public holidays 8am–1pm, 4–7pm; closed during church services; €2)*, which was abandoned in the 12C when the present church was built.

Santa Cecilia★ – *06 58 99 289. Open 9.30am–12.30pm, 4–7pm. Crypt €2.50.* A sanctuary dedicated to St Cecilia existed here in the 5C. In the 9C Pope Paschal I replaced it with a church, which has been much altered since. Inside, most of the medieval appearance is lost, although there is a 9C **mosaic**. The statue of **St Cecilia★** *(below the altar)* is by Stefano Maderno. **The Last Judgment★★★**, a masterpiece of medieval painting by Pietro Cavallini, was formerly

on the inside wall of the façade of the church and is now kept in the monks' chancel.

San Francesco a Ripa – This 17C church is notable for the statue of the Franciscan **Blessed Ludovica Albertoni★★** by Bernini in the fourth chapel in the left-hand aisle.

Piazza Santa Maria in Trastevere★★ – The heart of the district, this is probably the most charming corner of Trastevere, full of local color. The fountain at the center was remodeled by Bernini in 1659. On the left is the fine 17C façade of the **Palazzo di San Callisto**, next to the **Basilica di Santa Maria in Trastevere★★** *(see Major Churches)*.

In Piazza san Egidio the **Museo di Roma in Trastevere** *(06 06 08; www.museodiromaintrastevere.it; open daily 10am–8pm, last admission 7.30pm; closed Jan 1, May 1; €5.50)* occupies what was once the Convent of St Egidius in Trastevere. Displays reveal everyday life and fashion in 18C and 19C Rome. The popular Roman dialect poet Carlo Alberto Salustri, known as Trilussa, is commemorated by a monument in **Piazza Trilussa** opposite the **Sistine Bridge** (Ponte Sisto), named after its builder Sixtus IV.

Through the **Porta Settimiana**, one of the gates in the Aurelian Wall, is the **Villa Farnesina★★** *(06 68 02 73 97; www.lincei.it; open Jul–mid-Mar Mon–Sat 9am–1pm, mid-Mar–Jun 4pm; closed public holidays; €5)*, built between 1508 and 1511 for the great banker Agostino Chigi by Baldassarre Peruzzi. Its art collection is one of

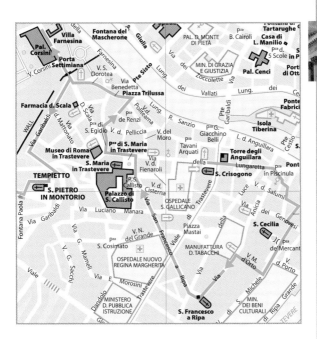

the gems of the Renaissance with works by Raphael, Giulio Romano, Sebastiano del Piombo, Peruzzi and Sodoma. The **Gabinetto Nazionale delle Stampe** *(06 69 98 01; open Mon–Sat 9am–1pm; archive open by appointment only)* houses an archive of prints and drawings from the 15C–19C.

Palazzo Corsini – Opposite the Villa Farnesina this 15C palace was rebuilt in the 18C by Ferdinando Fuga for Cardinal Corsini. It houses the **Galleria Nazionale d'Arte Antica** *(06 68 80 23 23. www.galleriaborghese.it; open Tue–Sun 8.30am–7.30pm; guided tours 9.30am, 11am, 12.30pm; closed Jan 1, May 1, Christmas; €4)*, also called the **Galleria Corsini**. This collection of mainly 17C and 18C paintings has notable works by Fra Angelico, Titian, and Caravaggio. Rome's botanic gardens, the **Orto Botanico**, were once the gardens of the Palazzo Corsini.

Back through the Porta Settimiana and along Via Garibaldi is the 15C church of **San Pietro in Montorio★**, built by Ferdinand II of Spain. The simple façade is typical of the Renaissance, as is the interior, notable for the **Flagellation★** *(first chapel on the right)* by Sebastiano del Piombo. Beatrice Cenci is buried beneath the high altar. In the courtyard, **Il Tempietto★★** was one of Bramante's first works after his arrival in Rome in 1499. Though tiny, the temple has the grandeur and rigorous conformity of a Classical building. Farther along Via Garibaldi you will find **Fontana Paola** *(see Green Guide Rome)*.

75

AROUND THE CITY WALLS

Built around AD 270, the city walls—the Aurelian Walls— enclosed the seven hills of Rome and Trastevere. Although today the city extends far beyond, they defined the city boundary and performed a defensive role until as late as the 19C.

PIAZZA DEL POPOLO★★

Ⓜ *Line A: Flaminio*

In the days of the Grand Tour, visitors to Rome arriving from the north would pass through the Porta del Popolo into the city. Now this grandiose square is the gateway to some of Rome's busiest shopping streets.

🐾 Walking Tour

✗ **Lunch stop** – Piazza del Popolo.

Piazza del Popolo★★ – This square was remodeled in the 19C by Giuseppe Valadier and is one of the largest in the city. It is linked to the gardens of **Il Pincio** *(see Green Rome)* by a series of terraces. The **Porta del Popolo★** in the 3C Aurelian Wall stands on the site of the ancient Porta Flaminia. The exterior façade was built in the 16C by Pius IV to impress visitors arriving from the north. The **obelisk** was brought from Heliopolis in the Augustan era and was originally set up in the Circus Maximus.

Santa Maria del Popolo★★ – This church is one of the first examples of the Renaissance style in Rome. Inside there is a wealth of **art treasures**. Above the altar in the **della Rovere Chapel** is a **fresco★** depicting the *Adoration of the Child* by Pinturicchio. The Baroque **Cybo Chapel** was designed by Carlo Fontana. The ceiling fresco is by

Pinturicchio, and the two elegant **tombs★** are by Andrea Sansovino.

The **Cerasi Chapel** houses two magnificent **paintings by Caravaggio★★★**, the *Conversion of St Paul* and the *Crucifixion of St Peter*. Above the altar is *The Assumption of the Virgin* by Annibale Carracci. The **Chigi Chapel★** was designed by Raphael. The dome mosaic dates from the Renaissance, as does the altarpiece. In the Baroque period, Bernini faced the base of the pyramid-shaped tomb of Agostino and Sigismondo Chigi with green marble and carved the figures of Daniel, the lion, Habakkuk, and the angel.

Museo di Hendrik Christian Andersen★ – 06 32 19 089. *www.museoandersen.beniculturali.it. Via Mancini 20. Open Tue–Sun 9am–7.30pm. Closed Jan 1, May 1, and Christmas.* To the north of Santa Maria del Popolo is Villa Helene, built by the Norwegian sculptor and painter Hendrik Christian Andersen at the beginning of the 20C as his residence and art studio. Now a museum, it houses 700 works, including sculptures, paintings, and graphic art.

Twin Churches – Carlo Rainaldi designed the two 17C churches at the south end of the square to provide a theatrical entrance to Via del Corso. Although they appear similar, they are in fact not symmetrical. The slightly earlier **Santa Maria di Montesanto** is elliptical beneath a 12-sided dome and **Santa Maria dei Miracoli** is circular, with an octagonal dome, and occupies a broader site.

Il Tridente – This is the name given to the trio of streets that diverge from Piazza del Popolo. **Via di Ripetta** follows the course of an ancient Roman road and contains many shops and boutiques. Following the route of the ancient Via Flaminia, **Via del Corso** runs in a straight line from Piazza del Popolo to Piazza Venezia. Handsome Renaissance palaces line this busy thoroughfare, Rome's main

shopping street. **Via del Babuino** was opened by Clement VII in 1525. It is named after the statue of Silenus next to the fountain by St Athanasius' church, which was discovered in such a hideous state that the Romans compared it to a baboon. Today the street is known for its antique shops.

Chiesa Anglicana (All Saints Anglican Church) – Designed by G. E. Street in the early 1880s in the English Gothic style. The spacious interior is enriched by a variety of Italian colored marble. The stained glass, depicting various saints and commemorating people connected with the church, is English.

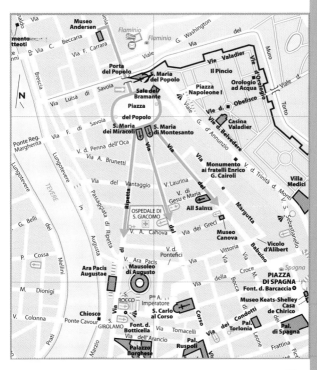

VIA VENETO★

M Line A: Barberini

Synonymous with glamor in the 1960s thanks to Fellini's movie *La Dolce Vita*, this district is no longer the meeting place of the famous but still has some of the smartest hotels and restaurants in the city.

🐾 Walking Tour

✕ **Lunch stop** – 🍴Via Vittorio Veneto.

Porta Pinciana – This gateway in the 3C Aurelian Wall was fortified in the 6C by Belisarius, Emperor Justinian's great general. **Via Vittorio Veneto**, created after 1879, runs through the heart of the beautiful Ludovisi district. Today it is mainly known for its luxury hotels, boutiques, and elegant cafés. The 19C **Palazzo Margherita** is now the United States Embassy.

Santa Maria della Concezione – *06 48 71 185. www.cappuccinivia veneto.it. Open 9am–noon, 3–6pm. The crypt is closed Thu.* This austere 1624 church of the Capuchin friars is notable for the **Cappuccini crypt★★** *(access on the right of the front steps)* where the friars prayed before bed. The bones and skulls of 4,000 people adorn this room, woven into Baroque artworks as a *memento mori*. Nearby is Bernini's **Fontana delle Api**, which incorporates the bees *(api)* from the influential aristocratic Barberini family's coat of arms, and his **Fontana del Tritone★** *(see Fabulous Fountains).*

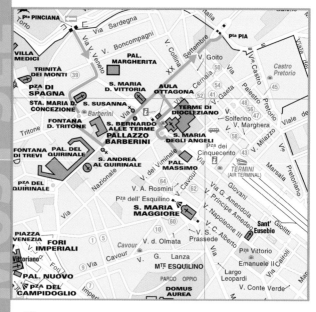

Palazzo Barberini★★ – This 17C Baroque palace was begun by Carlo Maderno, the main façade is the work of Bernini, and Borromini designed the oval spiral **staircase★** at the right-hand end of the front porch. The palace houses part of the **Galleria Nazionale d'Arte Antica★★** *(06 32 810; www.galleriaborghese. it; open Tue–Sun 8.30am–7.30pm; closed Jan 1 and Christmas. €5)*. The collection boasts a masterpiece by Raphael, **La Fornarina★★★**. The ceiling of the **Central Salon★★★** has a spectacular fresco by Pietro da Cortona. The second-floor rooms show Guido Reni's **Portrait of Beatrice Cenci★** and a fresco, the **Sleeping Putto★★**. Other famous works are the **Portrait of Henry VIII★★★** by Hans Holbein the Younger, the **Portrait of Erasmus★★★** by Quentin Metsys, and two works by Caravaggio, **Narcissus★★** and **Judith and Holofernes★**.

Santa Susanna★★ – *06 42 01 45 54. www.santasusanna.org. Open daily 9am–noon, 4–7pm. American church. Mass held in English, Sat 6pm, Sun 9am and 10.30am. Donations welcome.* The 16C **façade★★** of this church is a beautifully proportioned masterpiece by Carlo Maderno. The interior decoration is typical of the Mannerist style. Across the square **Santa Maria della Vittoria★★** *(open 6.30am–noon, 4.30–6pm)* was also designed by Maderno, though the simple lines of his **interior★★★** were richly decorated in Baroque style during the 17C. The **Cornaro Chapel**, designed by Bernini to resemble a theater, contains his astonishing **Ecstasy of St Theresa of Avila★★★**.

San Bernardo alle Terme – This church was created late in the 16C in a rotunda, formerly the southwest corner of the **Terme di Diocleziano** (Baths of Diocletian). These were built at the end of the 3C and were the largest and most beautiful in Rome. The church of **Santa Maria degli Angeli★★** *(see Major Churches)* was built on part of the site. The baths are also the location for the **Epigraphical and Prehistoric Museum★** *(06 39 96 77 00; open Tue–Sun 9am–7.45pm, last admission 7pm; closed Jan 1, May 1 and Christmas; €7)*, which houses a rich collection of ancient inscriptions and statues. Another part of the site houses the **Aula Ottagona★★★** *(see Major Museums)*.

Palazzo Massimo alle Terme★★★ *(see Major Museums)* – This is close to the **Stazione Termini**, Rome's main railway station, completed in 1950. **Via Nazionale** links Stazione Termini with Piazza Venezia and is one of the city's most important commercial centers. From Piazza della Repubblica heading northeast is **Via XX Settembre**, named after the date in 1870 when Italian troops entered the papal capital. The Ministry of Finance is home to the **Museo Numismatico della Zecca Italiana** *(06 47 61 33 17; www.museozecca.ipzs.it; open Tue–Sat 9am–12.30pm; closed Sat, Sun, Aug, and public holidays)*, which displays the currencies of every country in the world, including coins issued by the popes from the 15C. At the end of the street is the **Porta Pia** in the Aurelian Wall, whose spectacular inner **façade★** was designed by Michelangelo.

ESQUILINO★★★

Ⓜ *Line A: Vittorio Emanuele*

The largest of Rome's seven hills, the Esquilino had a somewhat disreputable reputation in ancient times. Although a little run-down in places today, it is a lively, multicultural area with a Chinatown and an array of cheap eateries. It has numerous churches, some dating back to early Christianity.

✱ Walking Tour

✕ **Lunch stop** – Piazza di S. Maria Maggiore.

Piazza dell' Esquilino – This gives a good **view★★** of the apse of **Santa Maria Maggiore★★★** *(see Major Churches)*. The Egyptian obelisk at the center of the square comes from the Mausoleum of Augustus. The 4C church of **Santa Pudenziana** is one of the oldest in Rome. It is on the site of a 2C bathhouse, the excavations of which are on display. The bell-tower dates from the 12C, as does the elegant doorway. The apse features a fine 4C **mosaic★**.

Santa Prassede★ – *Open daily 7am–noon, 4–6pm.* South of Santa Maria Maggiore, the 9C Santa Prassede church has Byzantine **chancel mosaics★** that show the figure of Christ flanked by St Peter and St Paul. **St Zenon's Chapel★★** was built between 817 and 824 by Pope Paschal I. The interior is covered in mosaics.

Arco di Gallieno – The Arch of Gallienus was erected in 262 in honor of the emperor, who was assassinated by Illyrian officers. It stands on the site of the Esquiline Gate in the Servian Wall.

Piazza Vittorio Emanuele II – The 19C square once hosted a daily market, now moved to the nearby Via Turati. In the north corner of the square are the ruins of a 3C fountain. The mysterious signs inscribed around the doorway of the **Porta Magica** have never been deciphered. The church of **Santa Bibiana** on Via Giovanni Giolitti was rebuilt in the 17C and was one of Bernini's first architectural projects. His **statue★** of St Bibiana is also an early work.

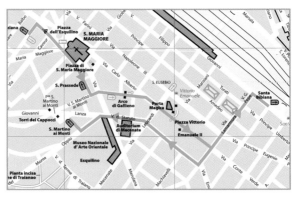

Upwardly mobile
By the time of Augustus, the Esquilino, which had been inhabited since the 8C BC, had acquired a rather seedy reputation. He transformed it to such an extent that it became a desirable area for aristocrats and emperors.

Auditorium di Mecenate – *06 06 08. Open Tue–Sat 9am–7pm (winter 5pm). Sun 9am–1pm. Closed Jan 1, May 1, Christmas. €2.60. Pre-booking required.* This is part of the luxurious 1C Villa of Maecenas, discovered in 1874. The underground structure, with its frescoes, was probably a *nymphaeum*, but Maecenas used it as an auditorium to receive his learned friends.

Museo Nazionale d'Arte Orientale – *06 46 97 48 32. www.museorientale.beniculturali.it. Open Tue–Fri 9am–2pm, Sat, Sun, & public holidays 9am–7.30pm. Closed Jan May 1, Christmas. €6.* On the *piano nobile* of Palazzo Brancaccio is the National Collection of Oriental Art whose extensive collections range from jewelery to documents and arms relating to the Near and Middle East.

San Martino ai Monti – *Book at least 10 days in advance by writing to Ufficio parrocchiale di S. Martino ai Monti, Via Monte Oppio 28, 00184 Roma, or call 06 47 84 701. Open Mon–Sat 9am–noon, 4–7pm.* Dedicated to St Martin, this church was founded in the 5C next to a 3C *titulus* in the house of Equitius. The church was completely transformed in the 17C.

CITTA UNIVERSITARIA

Ⓜ *Line B: Policlinico*

The University of Rome moved from its cramped accommodation in the Palazzo di Sapienza to this new campus in 1935. The main designer was Marcello Piacentini, a champion of "simplified Neoclassicism," who was also one of the architects of the EUR district. The chief interest of this lively area is the Basilica of St Lawrence.

San Lorenzo fuori le Mura★★ – *06 49 15 11. Open 7am–12.30pm, 3–6.30pm.* The church of St Lawrence without the Walls dates back to the 4C, when Constantine built a sanctuary for pilgrims coming to venerate the tomb of the martyr St Lawrence. The church was rebuilt in the 6C by Pope Pelagius II and underwent major alterations in the 13C under Pope Honorius III. Repairs after bomb damage during World War II aimed to restore its 13C appearance. Under the portico are several sarcophagi including the **"harvest" sarcophagus**★ carved in the 5C or 6C. Inside, the two distinct parts of the church are apparent, divided by the triumphal arch. Honorius's church has a nave and two aisles separated by beautiful granite columns of varying diameters. The floor and the two **ambones**★ are 13C Cosmati work. The present chancel was the nave of Pelagius's church. From the original nave only the tops of the 6C fluted columns are visible, supporting a magnificent sculpted architrave. The **bishop's throne**★ at the east end is by the Cosmati (1254). The 12C cloisters formed part of the fortified convent, since it was an easy target for thieves.

LATERANO★★★

Ⓜ *Line A: San Giovanni*

Once the residence of the popes, this district declined in importance after the 14C. After Italian unification a network of residential streets was laid out here to accommodate the increasing population.

Walking Tour

✕ **Lunch stop** – Via di S. Giovanni in Laterano.

Basilica di San Giovanni in Laterano★★★ *see Major Churches*

Piazza di San Giovanni in Laterano – The 15C BC Egyptian granite obelisk in the center of the square is the tallest in Rome. It was placed in the Circus Maximus in the 4C by Constantinus II and re-erected in its present position by Domenico Fontana.

Palazzo Lateranense – The Lateran Palace was the residence of the popes until 1309, when the papacy moved to Avignon. On their return the papal household moved to the Vatican. The present building was constructed in 1586 by Domenico Fontana. The palace is the headquarters of the Diocese of Rome, and houses the **Museo Storico Vaticano** *(06 69 88 63 86; http://mv.vatican.va; open Mon–Sat 9.30am–12.45pm, 1st Sun of the month 8.45am–1.45pm; closed Jan 1, Christian holidays; €5.)* The **Papal Apartment** contains ten rooms, each decorated with frescoes by late 16C artists. The **Historical Museum** celebrates the history of the papacy. Two features from the demolished medieval palace were preserved and reconstructed on the east side of the square. All that remains of the **banquet hall of Leo III** is an apse decorated with a mosaic, repaired in the 18C. The **Scala Sancta** *(06 77 26 641; check www.scalasancta.org for opening times)* according to tradition, came from Pontius Pilate's palace and had been used by Christ. The steps were relocated to a building specially designed by Fontana. At the top is the popes' chapel, known as the **Holy of Holies★★**. Above the altar is the famous icon of Christ called the **Acheiropoeton**, said to have been painted by St Luke and completed by an angel.

Santa Croce in Gerusalemme★ – *06 70 61 30 53. www.basilica santacroce.com. Open 7am–1pm, 2–6.30pm. The garden is open by appointment only.* In the 4C, Helen, the mother of Emperor Constantine, went on a pilgrimage to Jerusalem, and returned bearing a fragment of the True Cross. After her death Constantine converted part of the imperial Sessorian Palace into a church to house the precious relic. The

---

A grisly trial

In 897, the body of Pope Formosus was exhumed, clad in papal vestments, and seated on a throne for the Cadaver Synod. Accused of various transgressions relating to the church, the hapless corpse was found guilty. As punishment several of its fingers were cut off and the rest of the body was eventually thrown into the Tiber.

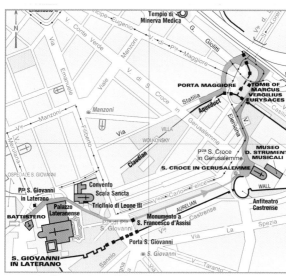

church acquired its present appearance in the 18C. The apse has an attractive 15C fresco by Antoniazzo Romano, illustrating the legend of the *Discovery of the Cross by St Helen*. The **Chapel of St Helen** is decorated with beautiful **mosaics★**, designed by Baldassarre Peruzzi. The statue above the altar is a Roman work originally representing Juno, but converted into St Helen. The **Chapel of the Holy Cross** and the **Relics Chapel** hold relics of the Passion that attract large numbers of pilgrims.

Museo degli Strumenti Musicali★ *see For Kids*

Anfiteatro Castrense – This amphitheater, like the Sessorian Palace, was probably part of the imperial properties in this district, and was incorporated into the 3C Aurelian Wall.

Porta Maggiore★ – This gate was built in the 1C AD to carry the Claudian Aqueduct across the Praenestina Way and the Labicana Way where it entered the city. In the 3C, the gate was incorporated into the Aurelian Wall. The demolition of a 5C bastion on the outside of the wall in the 19C revealed the **tomb of Marcus Vergilius Eurysaces★**, a rich baker who was also a freed slave. His enormous travertine tomb (dating from c 30 BC) has reliefs illustrating the different steps in breadmaking.

Claudian Aqueduct – Begun by Caligula and completed by Claudius in AD 52, this aqueduct brought water from the mountains near Subiaco, 42mi/68km from Rome. From Porta Maggiore, Nero built a branch channel to supply his **Domus Aurea★★** *(see p 48)*, traces of which still remain in the gardens of **Villa Wolkonsky**.

APPIA ANTICA★★

M *Line A: San Giovanni*

The Old Appian Way once extended all the way from Rome to the ports of the Adriatic, forming a link with the expanding Empire. Now it runs through a semi-rural oasis lined with ancient burial places.

🍴 Walking Tour

🍴 **Lunch stop** – Via Antica Appia.

Catacombe di Domitilla★★★ – *Entrance at Via delle Sette Chiese 282. 06 51 10 342. www.catacombe. roma.it. Guided tours only (35min). Open Wed–Mon 9am–noon, 2–5pm. Closed Tue, Jan 1, Easter, Christmas. €8.* This extensive network of galleries began as the private cemetery of Domitilla, whose uncle was Emperor Domitian. Many of the 1C and 2C tombs are not Christian. One of the oldest parts of the cemetery, the 2C **Flavian Vestibule**, is a long, wide gallery decorated with vine tendrils, birds, and cupids. Above the catacombs is the 4C **Basilica dei Santi Nereo e Achilleo**, which marked the graves of St Nereus and St Achilleus who were martyred under Diocletian. The saints' sarcophagi were moved to the Vatican in the 8C, and little remains of the original church.

Catacombe di San Callisto★★★ – *Via Appia Antica 110. 06 51 30 15 1. www.catacombe.roma.it. Guided tours only (45min). Open Thu–Tue 9am–noon, 2–5pm. Closed Jan 1, Feb, Easter, Christmas. €8.* Rome's first official Christian cemetery contains half a million tombs connected by over 12mi/20km of

tunnels. Most of the 3C popes are buried in the **Papal Crypt**, the oldest part of the cemetery. **St Cecilia's Crypt** was venerated in the 7C as the place of the saint's burial, before the discovery of her sarcophagus in the 9C and its subsequent removal to her church in Trastevere.

Catacombe di San Sebastiano★★★ – *06 78 87 035. www.catacombe.roma.it. Guided tours only (35min). Open Mon–Sat 9am–noon, 2–5pm. Closed mid-Nov–mid-Dec, Jan 1, Easter, Christmas. €8.* The three 1C mausoleums that stand here contain beautiful stucco decorations. In the 4C, a **basilica** was built above the catacombs, and subsequently rebuilt in the 17C for Cardinal Scipio Borghese. **St Sebastian's Chapel**, built in the 17C over his tomb, contains a statue of the saint by one of Bernini's pupils. Near the entrance to the catacombs is the **triclia**, where mourners met for a funeral meal. Graffiti on the walls invoking the Apostles Peter and Paul suggests that perhaps the saints' relics were lodged here temporarily during one of the persecutions.

Tomb motifs

Many tombs in the catacombs are decorated with motifs, which have a meaning. Among them are an anchor signifying hope, a dove with a twig in its beak symbolizing reconciliation between God and man, and a dolphin coming to the rescue of shipwrecked sailors indicating Jesus the Saviour.

Circo di Massenzio – *06 78 01 324. Via Appia Antica 153. Open Tue–Sun 9am–1pm. €2.60.* Emperor Maxentius built his Imperial residence beside the Appian Way, with a hippodrome for chariot races. The shape of the circus is well preserved. The **Tomba di Romolo** that was built for Maxentius's son Romulus in 309 is a domed rotunda with a *pronaos* reminiscent of the Pantheon.

Fosse Ardeatine – *06 51 36 742. Open daily 8.15am–5pm. Closed Jan 1, Easter, May 1, Aug 15, Christmas.* This memorial commemorates the massacre of 335 Romans by the SS in 1944 as a reprisal for an attack by the Resistance on German soldiers in Via Rasella. The tombs *(fosse)* of the victims are sheltered by a sanctuary and there is a museum of the Resistance next door.

Tomba di Cecilia Metella★ – *Via Appia Antica 161. 06 39 96 77 00. www.pierreci.it. Open Tue–Sun 9am–1hr before dusk. Closed Jan 1, Christmas. €6.* This iconic grave honors the wife of Crassus, one of Caesar's generals. From here the old road heads out through leafy countryside toward the 2C **Villa dei Quintili** *(06 39 96 77 00. www.pierreci.it; open Tue–Sun 9am–1hr before dusk; closed Jan 1 and Christmas. €6).*

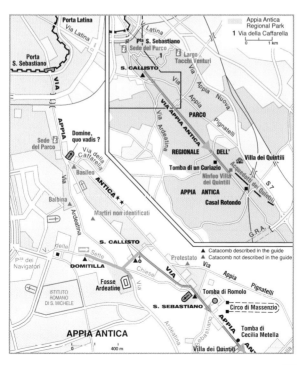

MAJOR MUSEUMS

Centuries of imperial and papal wealth are reflected in the richness of the city's museum collections, which feature artworks from antiquity to the Renaissance and beyond. For the **Vatican Museums★★★**, see p26.

Aula Ottagona★★★

See map on p 78. Entrance on Via Romita 8. 06 48 70 690. www.pierreci.it. Open Tue–Sun 9am–4pm. Closed Jan 1, Christmas.

Painted in the 1920s to resemble a planetarium, this wonderful domed octagonal room, originally part of the Baths of Diocletian, houses bronze and marble sculptures taken from Roman baths (2C–4C BC). Among the highlights of the collection are the **Pugilist Resting**, a superb figure cast in bronze from the Hellenistic period; **Venus Anadiomene**, depicting the goddess emerging from the waves; and **Hercules**, a fine example of an figure in motion.

Capitoline Museums★★★

See map on p 31. 06 39 96 78 00. www.museicapitolini.org. Open Tue–Sun 9am–8pm (ticket office 7pm), Dec 24 & 31 9am–2pm. Closed Jan 1, May 1, Christmas. €11, €13 joint ticket with Centrale Montemartini.

Opened to the public in 1734 by Clement XII, this 18C collection has changed little and ranks as one of the most important in Rome.

Palazzo Nuovo – The New Palace, built in 1654, is the work of Girolamo and Carlo Rainaldi. The noble 2C **statue of Marcus Aurelius★★** stands outside. The rooms in the museum feature sculpture from

the Imperial period, including portraits of the emperors and busts of poets and philosophers.

Don't miss:

- **Sala delle Colombe** The Dove Room takes its name from the fine **mosaic★★** that decorated Hadrian's villa at Tivoli.
- **Gabinetto della Venere** This charming room was built at the beginning of the 19C to house the **Capitoline Venus★★★**.
- **Salone** This room is the most typical of the museum. Note the two statues of **centaurs★★** and the **Wounded Amazon★**, a fine Roman copy of a statue sculpted by Polyclitus.
- **Sala del Fauno** Here stands the **Drunken Faun★★**, made from precious red marble and dating from Hadrian's reign.
- **Sala del Gladiatore** The sculpture in the middle is the **Dying Gaul★★★**, a Roman imitation of a 3C BC Greek bronze.

Palazzo Senatorio–Tabularium – An underground passage links the Palazzo Nuovo to the Palazzo dei Conservatori. It leads to the **Tabularium**, which housed the Roman archives in the 1C BC.

Palazzo dei Conservatori – Built in the 15C, it was substantially altered in 1568 according to Michelangelo's designs. As well as sculpture, it houses fine paintings from the 16C and 17C, and 18C tapestries and porcelain.

Don't miss:

- **Sala dei Trionfi** This houses the **Spinario★★**, a 1C BC bronze of a boy removing a thorn from his foot, and the magnificent 3C BC **bust of Junius Brutus★★**.

- **Sala della Lupa** Here is the Etruscan bronze of the **She-Wolf★★★**, which stood on the Capitol. It dates from the 5C BC; the twins are 15C additions.

- **Pinacoteca** Highlights here are the large painting by Guercino of **St Petronella★**, the **Gypsy Fortune-teller★★** by Caravaggio and his **St John the Baptist★★**, and the **Rape of the Sabine Women★★** by Pietro da Cortona.

Galleria Borghese★★★

Ⓜ *Line A: Flaminio. Piazzale Scipione Borghese 5. 06 32 810. www.galleriaborghese.it. Open Tue–Sun 8.30am–7.30pm. Closed Mon, Christmas. Visits are scheduled for 2hr. €8.50. Tickets must be collected at least 15min before entry.*

Cardinal Scipione Borghese was an avid collector of ancient, Renaissance, and Neoclassical art. He also commissioned some of the best-known sculptors of his time, such as Bernini and Cordier, as well as paintings from Caravaggio, Rubens, Reni, Guercino, and other great artists. The ground floor is devoted to sculpture and the picture gallery is on the upper floor.

Highlights:

- **Statue of Pauline Bonaparte★★★** This sculpture of Napoleon's sister posing half-naked as Venus caused a scandal, and her husband locked it away almost as soon as it was completed. It is now considered one of Canova's masterpieces.

- **Bernini Rooms★★★** The sculptures on display include *David*, *Apollo and Daphne*, and the *Rape of Proserpina*, one of Bernini's early commissions from Scipione.

- **Caravaggio Room★★★** This room houses six paintings by Caravaggio including *Madonna dei Palafrenieri*, intended for St Peter's Basilica, though it proved too radical and was banished to the Chiesa di Santa Maria dei Palafrenieri.

- **Works by Raphael★★★** The *Deposition* was commissioned

Capitoline She-Wolf, Palazzo dei Conservatori

B. Morandi/MICHELIN

MAJOR MUSEUMS

The Etruscans

This origin of the Etruscans is lost in prehistory. More advanced than their neighbors, the Etruscans governed Rome from the end of the 7C BC. Their domain stretched from Corsica to the Adriatic and from Capua to Bologna, but decline set in at the end of the 6C BC. Rome rebelled, expanded, and attacked their cities; in the 1C BC the Etruscans became Roman citizens. Traces of their civilization have mostly disappeared, but tombs reveal the grace and artistry of Etruscan ceramics and metalwork, and their elegant engineering, urban planning, and liberal social structure are becoming better appreciated.

by Atalanta Baglioni. The portrait of a *Lady with a Unicorn* is a fine example of Raphael's art, as is the *Portrait of a Man*.

- **The Danaë★★★** This painting by Correggio shows Zeus descending as a shower of gold.
- **Diana the huntress★★★** A masterpiece of the Baroque by Domenichino, as is his beautifully colored **Sibyl★**.
- **Portrait of a Man★★★** A finely detailed Renaissance work by Antonello de Messina.
- **Sacred and Profane Love★★★** This is an early work by Titian. His **Venus Tending Love**, in the same room, was painted when he was 75.

Museo Nazionale Etrusco di Villa Giulia★★★

Ⓜ *Line A: Flaminio. Piazzale di Villa Giulia 9. 06 32 01 951. Open Tue–Sun 8.30am–7pm. Closed Jan 1, Christmas. €4.*

This museum devoted to Etruscan civilization is housed in the summer villa of Pope Julius III, designed by Vignola in 1551. The sober façade is typical of this artist. The first courtyard is framed by a semicircular portico with **frescoed**

vaulting★, and in the main court-yard beyond is a Mannerist loggia and a *nymphaeum* adorned with caryatids, rockeries, and grottoes.

Highlights include:

- **Veii Sculptures★★★** These 6C BC terracotta sculptures of gods and heroes all come from the same temple.
- **Terracotta sarcophagus★★★** This dates from the end of the 6C and shows a husband and wife, reclining as if at a banquet, pursuing their life in the beyond.
- **The Antiquarium** These rooms are chiefly devoted to small **bronze objects★**. There are also ceramics, notably the **Chigi wine pitcher★★**, a superb example of Greek art from the middle of the 7C BC, and two **bucchero vases★** dating from the 6C BC.
- **Castellani Collection★** This superb collection includes many early Greek and Etruscan ceramics from the 8C BC to the Roman era.
- **Castellani Collection of Jewelry★** Over 2,500 pieces were gathered by the Castellani family of jewelers, dating from the 8C BC to the Roman and medieval periods.

- **Temples of Falerii Veteres★**
  Reconstructions of elements of
  these 4C BC buildings have been
  made from plans left by Vitru-
  vius, a 1C BC Roman architect.
  The **Bust of Apollo★** shows
  late Greek classical influence.
- **Praeneste: "Barberini" and
  "Bernardini" Tombs** The
  funerary artifacts from these
  rich tombs include carved ivory
  pieces, **gold jewelry★**, and
  decorative breastplates★★.
- **Ficoroni Cists★★★** Cists were
  marriage coffers, and this
  example is decorated with fine
  engravings of the Argonauts
  and hunting scenes.

Palazzo Altemps★★★

*See map on p 60. This palace,
along with Palazzo Massimo alle
Terme, the Terme di Diocleziano
(see p 79) and the Crypta Balbi (see
p 73), houses the Museo Nazionale
Romano. 06 39 96 77 00. www.
pierreci.it. Open Tue–Sun 9am–
7.45pm (last admission 6.45pm).
Closed Jan 1, May 1, Christmas.
€7. Guided tours and audio guides
(1hr 30min) in various languages.*

The palace was begun in about
1480 by Girolamo Riario, Sixtus IV's
nephew. It was later acquired by
Cardinal Marco Sittico Altemps,
who had it renovated by Martino
Longhi the Elder. The palace features some beautiful 15C and 16C
frescoes, of which the 15C **fresco★**
in the **Sala della Piattaia** is
outstanding. The museum houses
the sculpture collection of the 17C
Cardinal Ludovisi, which decorated
his villa in what is now Via Veneto.
Many of the ancient statues were
restored in the 17C by sculptors
such as Bernini and Algardi, so that
the collection is an unusual combination of the ancient original and
the Baroque restoration.

Don't miss:

- **Orestes and Electra★** This is
  the work of the Greek sculptor
  Menelaos and dates from the
  1C AD.
- **Ares Ludovisi★★** This sculpture, identified as Apollo, is a
  Roman copy of a statue from
  the Hellenistic period.
- **Ludovisi Throne★★★** This 5C
  BC Greek masterpiece is a throne
  for a cult statue and is decorated with reliefs. The main panel
  shows a young woman with
  two attendants, who shield her
  body with a veil. Archeologists

©Britta Jaschinski/APA Publications

Palazzo Altemps

have interpreted this scene as the birth of Aphrodite.

- **Painted Loggia★★** Commissioned at the end of the 16C, this fresco depicts a leafy garden.
- **Salone del Camino** The **Gaul taking his own life★★★**, a Roman copy of an original Greek bronze, dominates the center of the room, a magnificent example of Hellenistic art. The 3C **Grande Ludovisi sarcophagus★★** depicts battles between the Romans and the barbarians. The delicate face of the **Ludovisi Erinyes★** is emphasized by its dark base.

Palazzo Massimo alla Terme★★★

See map p 78. Ⓜ *Line A: Repubblica. Entrance on Largo Villa Peretti, at the end of Viale Einaudi. 06 48 90 35 00. www.pierreci.it. Open Tue–Sun 9am–7.45pm (last admission 6.45pm). Closed Jan 1, Christmas. €7 (also valid for other sections of the Museo Nazionale Romano).*

The Palazzo Massimo, built at the end of the 19C, used to be a Jesuit college and now houses the major part of the National Roman Museum's collection. Displayed on four floors, gold and ancient coins are in the basement, Greek and Roman statues on the ground and first floors, and frescoes and mosaics on the top floor.

Don't miss:
- **Statue of Augustus★★★** The emperor is shown dressed in the costume of the High Priest.
- **Gardens of Sallust** In Room VII there are some original Greek statues from this residential

Wounded Niobe

©Britta Jaschinski/APA Publications

district of the city, including the **Wounded Niobe★★★**, dating from 440 BC.

- **Young Girl from Anzio★★** The delicate sculpting of the girl's robe is noteworthy in this work from Nero's villa at Anzio.
- **Aphrodite Crouching★★★** This copy of a 3C BC Greek work shows the goddess bathing.
- **Lancellotti Discobolus★★★** This statue of a discus thrower is a fine copy of a classical Greek original. In the same room is the **Castelporziano Discobolus★**.
- **Sleeping Hermaphroditus★★** This is a graceful copy of a 4C BC Greek original.
- **Portonaccio Sarcophagus★** This tomb is carved with a powerful battle scene between the Romans and barbarians.
- **Acilia Sarcophagus★★** One of several sarcophagi in Room XIV, this tomb is elegantly decorated with carvings, illustrating a consular procession.
- **Triclinium from Livia's villa★★★** This reconstruction of the summer *triclinium* (dining room) from Livia's villa at Prima Porta has a beautiful fresco,

dating from 20–10 BC, showing a garden in full bloom.

- **Villa della Farnesina★★★** The marvelous stuccoes and paintings in this part of the museum come from a surburban villa dating from the Augustan era.
- **Gallery III** These rooms have mosaics dating from the end of the 1C BC to the 3C AD.
- **Numismatic Collection★★** This basement room displays coins from the 4C BC onward.

Galleria Doria Pamphili★★

See map p 64. Piazza Collegio Romano 2. 06 67 97 323. www.doriapamphilj.it. Open Fri–Wed 10am–5pm (last admission 4.15pm). Closed Jan 1, Easter, May 1, Aug 15, Christmas. €8.

Housed in one of Rome's largest palaces, built in the 15C and enlarged several times, this gallery has a fine collection of paintings and sculpture. The building retains many original features such as the 17C floor of the **Salla dei Velluti** and the Gobelin tapestries in the **Saletta Gialla**.

Highlights:

- **Flight into Egypt★★** A work by Annibale Carracci, the gentle but realistic landscape is characteristic of a taste that developed throughout the 17C.
- **The Usurers★** An important painting by Quentin Metsys.
- **Portrait of Innocent X★★★** This masterpiece by Velázquez shows the forbidding Giovanni Battista Pamphili after he became Pope. There is a **bust of Innocent X** by Bernini in the same room.

- **Rest after the Flight into Egypt★★★** This early work by Caravaggio is paired with his painting of **Mary Magdalene**.
- **Salome★★** This beautiful painting by Titian is the main focus of the 16C room.
- **Mourning the Death of Christ★★** This dramatic masterpiece by Hans Memling is in the 15C room.
- **Bust of Olimpia Maidalchini Pamphili★★** Algardi's sculpture captures the energy of the sister-in-law of Pope Innocent X.
- **Private Apartments★** Personal objects of the palace's owners are displayed here.

MAXXI (National Museum of XXI Century Arts)

Via Guido Reni, 4 A. 06 32 23 453. www.fondazionemaxxi.it. Open Tue–Sun 11am–7pm. 11€.

Rome's sensational new museum of ⬩**contemporary art**, designed by the Iraqi-born, London-based architect Zaha Hadid.

Galeria Doria Pamphili

MAJOR CHURCHES

As the center of Catholicism for two millennia, Rome has a wealth of churches, ranging from magnificent Renaissance basilicas to the humble foundations of early Christianity.

Chiesa del Gesù★★★

*See map p 69. 06 69 70 01.
www.chiesadelgesu.org. Open
7am–12.30pm, 4–7pm. Donations
welcome.*

The Chiesa del Gesù is the main Jesuit church in Rome and stands in Piazza del Gesù. Designed by Vignola in 1568, the majestic Latin-cross plan with its single broad nave was ideal for the Society's main purpose: preaching. The solemn **façade** by Giacomo della Porta, became a model for the "Jesuit style," often copied by Italian and foreign architects. The ornate Baroque decoration, added a century after the church was built, was intended to reinforce Roman Catholic doctrine against the ideas of the Reformation. Notable are the **Baciccia frescoes★★**, commissioned from Giovanni Battista Gaulli (known as "Il Baciccia") in 1672. The *Triumph of the Name of Jesus*, on the nave ceiling, was certainly his masterpiece, combining compositional technique with exuberant *trompe l'oeil*. The **Chapel of Sant'Ignazio di Loyola★★★**, where the remains of St Ignatius rest in a beautiful urn, was built by Andrea Pozzo, a Jesuit, between 1696 and 1700. On the sides of the altar, two groups of allegorical statues illustrate the work carried on by the Jesuits: on the left **Faith Triumphing over Idolatry** by Giovanni Théodon and on the right **Religion Vanquishing Heresy** by Pierre Legros. In the building to the right of the church are the rooms where **St Ignatius** lived and died *(access from Piazza del Gesù 45; 06 69 20 58 00; open Mon–Sat 4–6pm, Sun and public holidays 10am–noon; guided tours available, 30min)*. The ceiling and walls of the flanking passage are decorated all over with Pozzo's 17C *trompe l'oeil* frescoes.

Pantheon★★★

*See map p 64. 06 68 30 02 30.
Open Mon–Sat 8.30am–7.30pm,
Sun 9am–6pm. Closed Jan 1,
May 1, Christmas.*

This church was originally a temple dedicated to all the gods (hence its name). It was built by Marcus Agrippa, the great town planner, in 27 BC and destroyed by a fire in AD 80. Hadrian rebuilt it in its current form in the 2C AD. The Pantheon

---

The Jesuits

The Society of Jesus was founded in 1540 by Ignatius of Loyola (1491–1556), a Spanish soldier. The Society became the prime mover in the Counter-Reformation, which sought to rebut the Protestant teachings of John Calvin and Martin Luther. Jesuit missionaries and teachers were sent all over the world to win souls for Catholicism.

MUST SEE

Under the dome of Pantheon

©Dale Halbur/iStockphoto.com

was closed down by the first Christian emperors, together with all other places of pagan worship, and sacked by the barbarians in 410. The Emperor Phocas gave the Pantheon to Pope Boniface IV in 608 for use as a church, and it was restored early in the Renaissance. The **porch**, supported on 16 monolithic granite columns, is built on the foundations of Agrippa's temple, and the pediment bears an inscription with his name. Entering through a mighty bronze door, inside, the harmony and grandeur of the interior have an immediate impact. The diameter of the rotunda (142ft/43m) is equal to its overall height. The astonishing **antique dome★★★** was built by pouring concrete over a temporary wooden framework. This technology was lost in the Middle Ages, and rediscovered by Renaissance artists like Bramante and Michelangelo through study of the Pantheon's dome. At the center of the coffered ceiling is an enormous round opening *(oculus)*, which lights the interior. Around the walls are chapels and shrines to the kings of modern Italy, including the **tomb of Victor Emmanuel II** (1820–78). Another shrine contains the **tomb of Raphael**, who died in 1520 aged 37.

San Giovanni in Laterano★★★

See map p 83. 06 77 20 79 91. Open 7am–6.30pm. Free except cloisters €2.

This is the cathedral of Rome. The first basilica was built by Constantine in the 4C, and was rebuilt several times. The present building retains the original plan, but dates in the main from the 17C.

What's outside?

+ **Main façade** This is the major work of Alessandro Galilei (1691–1736), a Baroque architect. On the roof are huge statues of Christ and the saints. The **statue of Constantine** in the porch comes from the Imperial Baths on the Quirinal. The bronze doors are from the Curia in the Forum.
+ **Cloisters★** *06 77 20 79 91. Open daily 9am–6pm. €2.* These 13C cloisters feature twisted marble columns with varied capitals and a mosaic frieze.
+ **Baptistry★** – *Entrance in Piazza S. Giovanni in Laterano.* Built in the 4C and much restored in the Renaissance. The adjoining **chapels** have fine 5C mosaics.
+ **North façade** This was added by Domenico Fontana in 1586. In the porch is a bronze **statue of Henri IV** of France.

What's inside?

+ **Nave and aisles** Designed around 1650 by the great Baroque architect Borromini. The **ceiling★★** was begun by Pius IV in 1562; his arms are in the center. The **statues of the Apostles★** are by some of Bernini's followers.

- **Corsini Chapel★** Alessandro Galilei was also responsible for this chapel built on the Greek-cross plan beneath a dome. The fragment of heavily restored **fresco**, attributed to Giotto, shows Boniface VIII announcing the Jubilee Year in 1300.
- **Transept** This was renovated in about 1565 by Giacomo della Porta and is elaborately adorned with frescoes, marble, and gilding. The ostentatious **ceiling★★**, bearing the arms of Clement VIII, is rich in color and gilding and was designed by Taddeo Landini (late 16C). The pediment in the chapel of the Holy Sacrament is supported by four beautiful **Antique columns★** in gilded bronze, the only ones of this kind in Rome.
- **Apse** This was substantially altered in the 19C, but it retains the 5C mosaic that had already been restored in the 13C by Jacopo Torriti.
- **Museo della Basilica** *Right of the chancel. 06 77 20 79 91. Open daily 9am–6pm. €1.* The basilica's museum displays a number of reliquaries, chalices, and other liturgical objects.

San Giovanni in Laterano
©World Pictures/Photoshot

Santa Maria Maggiore★★★

See map p 80. 06 48 31 95.
Open 7am–7pm.

The original church was built by Sixtus III in the 5C, and in spite of alterations throughout the subsequent centuries, the interior, with its almost perfect proportions and two rows of Ionic columns, remains a striking example of early Christian architecture.

What's outside?

- **Main façade** The central porch is flanked by two identical wings, although more than a century separates the construction of the one on the right (1605) and the one on the left (1721–43). The Romanesque campanile dates from the 14C and is the highest in Rome.
- **Loggia mosaic★** *Access by the steps on the left of the porch.* The upper part showing Christ, the Virgin, and the saints is the work of Filippo Rusuti (late 13C). Below are **four scenes★** showing the legend of the founding of the basilica. The graceful lines, richly appareled figures, and fine perspectives are reminiscent of the Florentine style of Cimabue and Giotto.
- **Apsidal façade** – This was designed by Carlo Rainaldi in the 17C to integrate the domes of the Pauline and Sistine chapels with the apse of the basilica.

What's inside?

- **Mosaics★★★** The 5C mosaics in the nave and on the chancel arch depict scenes from the Old and New Testament. Those in the nave are among the oldest

Santa Maria Maggiore

Christian mosaics in Rome, and are incomparable. The chancel arch dates from the 5C and its mosaics show Byzantine influence and are probably later than those in the nave.

* **Apse** The dazzling mosaics here comprise elements taken from a 5C mosaic, transformed at the end of the 13C by Jacopo Torriti when Nicolas IV rebuilt the apse.
* **Ceiling★** The 15C coffered ceiling is possibly the work of Giuliano da Sangallo, and was decorated with the first gold to come from Peru, which was

The legend of the snow
In 356 the Virgin appeared to Pope Liberius and told him to build a church on a site to be marked by a fall of snow. Although it was August, snow was found on the Esquiline, and plans were made to build a church on the spot. The miracle is celebrated on August 5 each year when a shower of white rose petals rains down on the congregation.

given to Pope Alexander VI by Ferdinand and Isabella of Spain.

* **Tomb of Cardinal Consalvo Rodriguez** This Gothic tomb has magnificent marble decoration.
* **Cappella di Sisto Quinto** This chapel was built for Sixtus V by Domenico Fontana, and is almost a church in itself. Designed on the Greek-cross plan beneath a dome painted with frescoes, it is resplendent with gilding, stucco, and marble. The chapel contains the monumental tombs of Sixtus V and Pius V.
* **Cappella Sforza** The highly original architectural style of this chapel is the work of Giacomo della Porta, probably from designs by Michelangelo.
* **Cappella Paolina** Also known as The Borghese Chapel after the family name of Pope Paul V, who commissioned it, this is identical in plan to Sixtus V's chapel but with even more sumptuous decoration. The main altar is set with jasper, lapis lazuli, agate, and amethyst. The chapel contains the tombs of Clement VIII, cardinal protector of England, and of Paul V himself.

95

Cloisters, San Paolo Fuori le Mura

J. Rolland/Michelin

San Clemente★★

See map p 47. Entrance into south aisle from Via di S. Giovanni in Laterano. Lower basilica: 06 77 40 021. www.basilicasanclemente. com. Open 9am–12.30pm, 3–6pm. Closed Christmas. €3.

This church was founded in the 4C in a private house belonging to a Christian and is one of the oldest Roman basilicas. Ruined in 1084, it was rebuilt on the same site by Paschal II in 1108. The main entrance through an atrium shows the simple austerity of medieval buildings. The interior retains its 12C basilica plan with a nave and two aisles divided by recycled ancient columns, though there are some 18C frescoes. The **Cosmati floor** (12C) is one of the best preserved in Rome. The vividly colored and beautiful **apse mosaic★★★** shows the the Crucifixion, with12 doves symbolizing the Apostles, flanked by the Virgin and St John. St Catherine's Chapel is decorated with **frescoes★** by Masolino da Panicale.
The **lower basilica** is accessed via steps in the north aisle and

consists of a narthex, a nave and two aisles, and an apse. The **frescoes★** here are from the 11C and 12C, though some date back as far as the 9C. Those in the nave are accompanied by ancient cartoon captions, an extremely rare example of the transition from classical to vulgar Latin. Beneath the 4C basilica are the remains of **two houses** built in Republican times. The one beneath the apse was converted in the 3C into a *mithraeum*, a small temple for the cult of the god Mithras.

San Paolo Fuori le Mura★★

Ⓜ *Line B: Basilica S. Paolo. Via Ostiense 186. Enter by the main door from Viale di S. Paolo. 06 69 88 08 00. www.annopaolino.org. Open daily 7am–6.30pm (winter 6pm). Cloisters: 9am–1pm and 3–6.30pm (winter 6pm).*

St Paul Without the Walls attracts visitors and pilgrims from all over the world. After he was beheaded St Paul was buried beside the Via Ostiensis, which was lined with tombs, as were all the major roads leading out of Rome. In the 4C, Emperor Constantine built a basilica over the tomb. At the end of the 4C a new and greatly enlarged basilica was constructed, bigger at the time than St Peter's. The greatest artists were employed to embellish the basilica, from Pietro Cavallini and Arnolfo di Cambio to Carlo Maderno. In 1823 St Paul's Basilica was almost entirely destroyed by fire, and the reconstruction has only fragments of the original church.

Don't miss:

◆ **Nave★★★** Eighty granite pillars divide the nave and four aisles. The gold and white coffered ceiling bears the arms of Pope Pius IX (1846–78), who consecrated the reconstructed basilica.

◆ **Baldacchino★★★** The fine marble canopy over the altar is a 13C Gothic work by Arnolfo di Cambio, and is decorated with many skilfully executed figures.

◆ **Chapel of the Holy Sacrament★** This 17C chapel by Carlo Maderno contains a 14C wooden crucifix and a wooden statue of St Paul dating from the 14C.

◆ **Paschal candlestick★★** This remarkable piece of 12C Romanesque art by Nicolà di Angelo and Pietro Vassalletto is decorated with monsters and scenes from the life of Jesus.

◆ **Cloisters★** These survived the 19C fire and are considered among the most beautiful in Rome. They were probably built by a member of the Vassalletto family (13C) and feature a variety of inlaid marble columns and a mosaic frieze above the arcades.

Abbazia delle Tre Fontane★ – 🅜 *Line B: Laurentina. From Via Laurentina a drive leads to Three Fountains Abbey. 06 54 01 655. www.abbaziatrefontane.it. Open daily 6.30am–12.30pm, 3–8.30pm.* A few miles south of San Paolo Fuori le Mura, this abbey is on the site where St Paul supposedly died. Surrounded by green hills and with the scent of eucalyptus trees in the air, a small group of buildings now stands here. In addition to the abbey, a convent and three churches occupy this peaceful spot, which has been a pilgrim destination since the Middle Ages. **Santa Maria Scala Coeli** was built in 1583 by Giacomo della Porta to an octagonal plan beneath a dome. **Santi Vincenzo e Anastasio alle Tre Fontane** is the 13C abbey church of the Trappist monks who have occupied the neighboring monastery since 1868. **San Paolo alle Tre Fontane** was designed in the 16C by Giacomo della Porta to replace two chapels. A building commemorating St Paul's martyrdom stood here from the 5C.

St Paul
According to legend, St Paul was martyred when he was beheaded at Abbazia delle Tre Fontane. Once the blow had been struck, his head fell to the ground and bounced three times. Springs or fountains then spurted out of the ground in miraculous fashion at each place where his head had bounced, the "tre fontane" (three fountains) that are now commemorated in the abbey's name.

Santa Maria degli Angeli★★

M *Line A: Termini. Entrance in Piazza della Repubblica. 06 48 80 812. www.santamariadegliangeli-roma.it. Open daily 7am–6.30pm.*

In 1561 Pius IV decided to convert the ruined **Terme di Diocleziano** into a church and a Carthusian monastery. Michelangelo, by then 86 years old, was put in charge, and his design closely followed the architecture of the original baths. Extensive reconstruction in the 18C by the Neapolitan architect Vanvitelli has left little of this original church, though there is an exhibition in the sacristy that gives a detailed account of the original design. In the early 20C the 18C façade was demolished, revealing the unusual unadorned curved wall of the *calidarium* of the original baths. The church's **vestibule** was the *tepidarium* of the baths. Between the vestibule and the transept is a statue of St Bruno, the founder of the Carthusian order. The **transept★** gives the best idea of the solemn majesty of the

ancient building. It occupies the central bath hall, with its eight monolithic granite columns, and is decorated with a number of paintings, mostly 18C works. Many of these came from St Peter's where they were replaced by mosaics. Like the transept, the chancel is generously decorated with paintings, the most notable being **The Martyrdom of St Sebastian** by Domenichino, and **The Baptism of Jesus** by Carlo Maratta. The **Great Cloisters**, which belonged to the monastery are attributed to Michelangelo.

Santa Maria in Cosmedin★★

See map p 71. **M** *Line B: Circo Massimo. Piazza della Bocca della Verità 18. 06 67 81 419. Open summer daily 9am–4.30pm.*

This fine medieval church is on the site of a 6C grain distribution center. In the 8C an oratory in one of the storehouses was enlarged by Pope Hadrian I and became the church for the Greeks who had settled in the area between the Aventine and the Tiber. Early in the 12C the porch and soaring **campanile★** were added by Popes Gelasius II and Callistus II. The campanile, with its bold arcading, is one of the most elegant in Rome. The marble disk in the porch known as the **Bocca della Verità** is a 4C BC drain cover, possibly from the nearby Temple of Hercules. The beautiful floor and marble furnishings, including the **baldacchino** over the high altar, are all Cosmati work. The church was restored to its medieval appearance in the 19C when a baroque façade was removed.

Santa Maria degli Angeli

G. Bludzin/MICHELIN

Bocca della Verità, Santa Maria in Cosmedin

Santa Maria in Trastevere★★

See map p 75. 06 58 14 802. www.santamariaintrastevere.org. Open daily 7.30am–8pm.

The 3C Pope Calixtus I is said to have built the first sanctuary on this site, but the present basilica is the work of Pope Innocent II in the 12C. As with all medieval Roman buildings, the 22 granite columns dividing the nave from the aisles were taken from ancient monuments; all are crowned with classical capitals in either the Ionic or the Corinthian orders.

What's outside?

- **Campanile** This dates from the 12C; a small recess at the top is decorated with a mosaic of the Virgin and Child, to whom the basilica is dedicated.
- **Façade** The mosaic on the façade (12C–13C) shows the Virgin and Child flanked by a procession of women who are carrying lamps.
- **Porch** Carlo Fontana remodeled the porch early

in the 18C. It contains two 15C frescoes depicting the Annunciation. The statues of the saints on the balustrade over the porch were erected from the 17C to the 18C.

What's inside?

- **Chancel mosaics★★★** The 12C mosaics on the chancel arch show the Prophets Isaiah and Jeremiah and the symbols of the Evangelists. Those in the half-dome of the apse, also 12C, show Christ and the Virgin surrounded by saints, and display Byzantine influence. The mosaics between the windows and at the base of the chancel arch illustrate scenes from the life of the Virgin, and are fine late 13C works by Pietro Cavallini.
- **Avila Chapel** This 17C chapel and its dome are the exuberant creation of Antonio Gherardi, and feature Baroque *trompe l'oeil* decoration.
- **Tabernacle** Among the treasures of this church is the charming late 15C wall tabernacle by Mino da Fiesole.

FABULOUS FOUNTAINS

Rome's fountains are almost as famous as its churches. Some mark the termini of aqueducts, some adorn the elegant squares of the Roman nobility, and some simply offer a cooling drink on a hot day.

Fontana dei Fiumi★★★

See map p 63. Piazza Navona.

The Fountain of the Rivers, at the center of the square, was created by Bernini for Pope Innocent X in 1651. The Baroque architect created a pile of rockwork, hollowed into grottoes and crowned by an obelisk dating from the reign of Domitian, which had been found on Via Appia. The four marble statues represent four rivers, symbolizing the quarters of the world: the Danube for Europe, the Nile for Africa, the Ganges for Asia, and the Plate for America. The rigidity and symmetry of the obelisk contrasts strikingly with the fluid lines of the base, where the wind seems to tear at the trees as the marble statues gesticulate. At the southern end of the square is the **Fontana del Moro**, built at the end of the 16C. Bernini designed the

central figure of the Moor and one of his pupils was responsible for the vigorous setting. The **Fontana del Nettuno** at the other end of the square was moved here at the end of the 16C. The statue of the sea god Neptune and those around it date from the 19C.

Fontana di Trevi★★★

See map on p 53. Piazza di Trevi.

This late Baroque fountain, one of Rome's most famous monuments, is an impressive sight, made all the more striking by its position in a tiny piazza. It was commissioned from Nicolà Salvi by Clement XII in 1732 to adorn the end of the *Acqua vergine*, an aqueduct built by Marcus Agrippa in 19 BC. The theatrical fountain is built in the style of a commemorative arch and fills the whole width of the façade. The

Fontana di Trevi

© S. Greg Panosian/iStockphoto.com

Fontana della Barcaccia and the Spanish Steps

J. Malburet/MICHELIN

central figure, Neptune, rides in a chariot drawn by sea horses and two tritons, and the coins thrown in the water reflect the tradition that one coin (cast backward, over the left shoulder) ensures a return to Rome, two bring love, and three a wedding in the Eternal City. You should, however, be wary of pickpockets and pushy flower sellers here.

Fontana del Tritone★

See map on p 78. Piazza Barberini.

Bernini's lively Triton Fountain (c 1642) has four dolphins supporting an open scallop shell, on which a triton sits blowing a column of water upward through a conch shell. Between the dolphins' tails are the keys of St Peter and the Barberini coat of arms belonging to Pope Urban VIII, with its signature bees.

Fontana della Barcaccia★

Piazza di Spagna.

The Boat Fountain at the foot of the Spanish Steps was designed

by Bernini's father, Pietro, in 1627 for Pope Urban VIII. Because the water pressure here was too low to support spectacular cascades, the sculptor instead designed a leaky boat, half-submerged in a pool of water. Allegedly, he was inspired by a boat stranded in Piazza di Spagna by flood waters. At either end the boat is decorated with the suns and bees of the Barberini coat of arms.

Fontana delle Tartarughe★

See map on p 71. Piazza Mattei.

This charming late Renaissance work is by Taddeo Landini, probably from a design by Giacomo della Porta. Legend tells how Duke Mattei, after gambling away his fortune, had the fountain built overnight to prove that, even when ruined, a Mattei could still achieve wonders. The turtles being assisted into the basin by four youths, which give the fountain its name are not in fact contemporary, but were added nearly a century after it was built.

GREEN ROME

If you find that the sheer amount of art and architecture and history on show is becoming overwhelming, Rome has plenty of peaceful green spaces where you can unwind and prepare for the next gallery.

Gardens of Villa Borghese

D.Chapuis/MICHELIN

Borghese Gardens★★

Ⓜ *Line A: Flaminio*

Villa Borghese and its surrounding parkland were designed for Cardinal Scipione Borghese, the nephew of Pope Paul V, in the early 17C. The garden was the first of its kind in Rome, planted with 400 fragrant umbrella pines, and featuring sculpture by Bernini's father, Pietro, and water features by Giovanni Fontana. It became the property of the Italian state in 1901 and is now the largest and most famous of Rome's public parks. The park is 3.5mi/5.5km in circumference and contains flower gardens set with Neoclassical sculpture, imitation temples and other follies, fountains, a 17C aviary, the disappointing Museo di Zoologia, and a riding school. It is also home to three important art galleries and the 🐾 **Bioparco**, a new zoo where the emphasis is on conservation. Bicycles to rent.

Highlights:

◆ **Villa Borghese★★★** This little palace, which houses the **Galleria Borghese★★★** *(see Major Museums)*, was designed in 1613 by Flaminio Ponzio and is a delightful example of a rich prelate's house. During a late 18C restoration, the highly ornate southwest façade (the present front entrance) was stripped of some decoration and the steps were altered. The villa has a portico from which four statues look down.

◆ **Galleria Nazionale d'Arte Moderna★★** *Viale delle Belle Arti 131. 06 32 29 82 21. www. gnam.arti.beniculturali.it. Open Tue–Sun 8.30am–7.30pm. Closed Jan 1, Christmas. Guided tours available (1hr) in various languages. €10.* Housed in a lovely building built in 1911 by Cesare Bazzani for the International Exhibition, this gallery is primarily dedicated to 19C and 20C painting and sculpture, mostly by Italian artists. The 19C Italian galleries are arranged according to schools, and there are also works by Cézanne, Degas, Monet, and Van Gogh. The 20C galleries have displays on the Futurists, Dadaists, and Surrealists, and include works by Klimt, Modigliani, de Chirico, Duchamp, and Mondrian. The gallery also accommodates temporary exhibitions and has an excellent **café** that is open to passers-by as well as gallery visitors.

- **Seahorse Fountain** This was commissioned in 1791 by Prince Marcantonio Borghese, who renovated the gardens.

- **Piazza di Siena** This grassy amphitheater is named after the native town of the Borghese. Set among umbrella pines, it now hosts international equestrian events.

- **Temple of Diana** This tiny round Neoclassical temple stands at the end of the Viale dei Pupazzi.

- **Giardino del Lago** This is one of the most popular corners of the park, planted with magnolias, aloe, and yucca. The lake reflects the columns of the little **Temple of Aesculapius** on an island in the middle, and there are row boats for hire.

- **Viale delle Belle Arti** Beginning with the **Museo Nazionale Etrusco di Villa Giulia**★★★ *(see Major Museums)*, this avenue is lined with national pavilions that were built for the International Exhibition in 1911. One of these is the **British School at Rome** (Scuola Britannica d'Arte), designed by Edwin Lutyens, whose façade is based on that of St Paul's Cathedral. Originally a school of archeology, this is now a research institute which brings artists, architects, and scholars to the Eternal City, and offers public lectures on alternate Wednesdays.

Parco dell'Appia Antica★★

See map p 85.

The atmospheric, tree-lined Via Appia Antica was known in antiquity as the "Queen of Roads." Paved with polygonal basalt flagstones, it runs in a straight line for several miles southeast from the city. The fields on either side are full of the remains of ancient tombs and monuments. The park is best

J. Rolland/MICHELIN

Parco dell'Appia Antica

GREEN ROME

103

View from Gianicolo

© Ivan Liakhovenko/Dreamstime.com

explored by bicycle, and these can be hired from the **Sede del Parco**, where there is an information point. There are also guided bicycle tours. The park is closed to cars on Sundays.

The Aventine★

See map p 42.

The Aventine is a tranquil residential district with several green spaces. The **Giardino degli Aranci** (Parco Sarello) has a good **view★** across the river to Trastevere. The **Rosete di Roma**, near the church of Santa Prisca, is open exclusively from end-April to end-June when the roses are in bloom.

Gianicolo★

The Janiculum Hill has often played a part in the defense of the city, and Garibaldi and his Republicans held off a superior French force for weeks here in 1849 during the struggle for Italian unification. The road that winds along the crest of the hill beneath the umbrella pines has numerous monuments to Garibaldi and his men, and offers fine **views**.

Don't miss:

♦ **Fontana Paola** This fountain in the shape of a commemorative arch was commissioned by Pope Paul V. In summertime, outdoor stages colonize the area and an impromptu café sprawls across the road.

♦ **Monumento a Giuseppe Garibaldi** The dashing and charismatic Garibaldi led his troops in many of the battles that unified Italy. Emilio Gallori's grandiose statue (1895), shows the hero on horseback. Garibaldi made great efforts to reduce the temporal power of the papacy, and in 1929 the Vatican requested that the statue be turned around, so that he was no longer glaring at St Peter's.

♦ **Monumento ad Anita Garibaldi** Garibaldi's Brazilian wife, who often fought beside him, has a much better monument. Astride a rearing horse, she carries a baby and a pistol. Anita died—ill, pregnant, and in Giuseppe's arms—after the 1849 retreat. Eleven years later, when Garibaldi rode to hail

Victor Emanuel II as king of Italy, he wore Anita's striped scarf over his grey poncho.

- **Manfredi lighthouse** This was built in 1911 and was a gift to the city from Italians in Argentina.
- **Sant'Onofrio** *Piazza di Sant'Onofrio 2. 06 68 64 498. Open Tue–Sun 10am–noon. Closed Aug.* This church was founded in 1434, and it has retained the simple appearance of a hermitage. On the right of the main door are frescoes by Domenichino, illustrating the life of St Jerome (1605). The attractive frescoes in the **apse★** were probably painted by Baldassarre Peruzzi assisted by Pinturicchio.

Il Pincio

See map p 77.

The Pinci family, which had a garden here in the 4C, has left its name to this little hill, still covered by one of the most delightful gardens in Rome. The Pincio was laid out in its present style during the Napoleonic occupation (1809–14), according to designs by Giuseppe Valadier, and it became a fashionable place to stroll. Magnificent umbrella pines, palm trees, and evergreen oaks shade the zig-zagging avenues. From the terrace of Piazzale Napoleone I, there is a magnificent **view★★★**, particularly at dusk.

Don't miss:

- **Water clock** This was built in 1867 by a Dominican monk, Giovan Battista Embriago, and presented at the Universal Exhibition in Paris in 1889.

- **Obelisk** Halfway along Viale dell'Obelisco, which leads to the gardens of the Villa Borghese, stands an obelisk, found near the Porta Maggiore in the 16C. It was originally erected by Emperor Hadrian in memory of his young friend Antinoüs.
- **Cairoli Monument** This commemorates two brothers, Enrico and Giovanni, Italian patriots who fought beside Garibaldi and died in 1867.
- **Casina Valadier** This exclusive restaurant was popular with the famous well into the 20C, and was patronized by Mussolini, Gandhi, and Richard Strauss.

Villa Celimontana

See map p 47.

This piece of land was bought by the Dukes of Mattei in 1553, who converted the vineyard slopes into a formal garden. **Villa Celimontana**, formerly Villa Mattei, houses the Italian Geographical Society. The garden now belongs to the city and is a popular place for picnics. In summer it hosts a **jazz festival**; in winter there is an ice rink.

Villa Doria Pamphili

Via di S. Pancrazio. This road is very busy, so visitors with small children should take care.

This vast public park surrounds a 17C country house, the **Casino del Bel Respiro**, which is decorated with statues and sculptures and set among terraces. This is a popular place for picnics, and also has grotto-fountains, several glasshouses, an 18C lake, and playgrounds.

GREEN ROME

105

EXCURSIONS

If you are making an extended visit there are churches and parks on the outskirts of the city to explore. Farther afield you will find the country retreats of the ancient Roman nobility.

Tivoli★★★

19mi/31km east of Rome.

The lively and picturesque town of Tivoli to the east of Rome retains some traces of the past. The cathedral, rebuilt in the 17C and flanked by a 12C Romanesque campanile, contains a fine group of 13C carved wooden figures depicting the **Deposition★**.

Hadrian's Villa★★★ – *3.5mi/6km below the town: about 1mi/1.5km off the highway, turn right onto Via Rosolino. Parking lot by the ticket booth. Tivoli–Rome buses stop on request. 06 39 96 79 00. www.villa adriana.com. Open daily 9am–1hr before dusk (last ticket half an hour before closing). Closed Jan 1, May 1, and Christmas. €6.50.* Probably the richest building project in antiquity, the estate was designed largely by Emperor Hadrian himself as a summer retreat from the affairs of state. He created an open-air museum of Roman architecture, with reproductions of his favorite Classical buildings. The villa fell into disrepair after the 6C. Since 1870, the site has belonged to the Italian government. The design of the villa is so unusual that archeologists have not been able to identify the buildings or their uses with any certainty. The present entrance is probably not the one used in Hadrian's day. Before you explore the villa, you might like to study the model that is on display in the building next to the parking lot.

Highlights:

- ◆ **Stoa Poikile★★** Only the north wall remains of this portico, based on an original in Athens.
- ◆ **Maritime Theater★★★** This circular construction consists of a portico and a central building. It is surrounded by a canal spanned by swing bridges.
- ◆ **Baths★★** The Small Baths and the Great Baths both show high architectural standards.
- ◆ **Museo** The museum contains the results of the most recent excavations.
- ◆ **Canopus★★★** The route to Canope from Alexandria was a canal lined with temples and gardens. Hadrian had part of his estate landscaped to look like the Egyptian site, with a canal at the center and a copy of the Temple of Serapis at one end.
- ◆ **Imperial Palace** This complex extended from the Piazza d'Oro to the libraries. The **Piazza d'Oro★★** was a rectangular area surrounded by a double portico. The **Doric Pillared Hall★★** takes its name from the surrounding portico, which was composed of pilasters with Doric bases. Adjoining the Pillared Hall is a huge section of curved wall that may have been part of a summer dining room. On one side of the library court is an infirmary whose **floor★** is paved with fine mosaics. The ruins of the library buildings are on the north side of the courtyard.

Villa d'Este★★★ – *In the center of Tivoli, down the street from Largo Garibaldi. 19 97 66 166. www.villadestetivoli.info. Open Tue–Sun 8.30am–1hr before dusk. Closed Jan 1, May 1, Christmas. €6.75.* This Renaissance pleasure garden and its villa were built for Cardinal Ippolito d'Este in 1550. The simple architecture of the villa contrasts with the elaborate gardens (7.5 acres/3ha), which descend in a series of terraces on the western slope of the hill. In their heyday over 300gal/1,200l of water per second flowed through the system that fed the fountains.

Highlights:

- **Sala grande** The Salon is decorated in the Mannerist style by pupils of Girolamo Muziano and Federico Zuccari. On the ceiling is a fresco of the **Banquet of the Gods**.
- **Viale delle Cento Fontane★★★** The hundred fountains that line this avenue take the form of small boats, obelisks, animal heads, eagles, and lilies, the latter recalling the Este coat of arms.

- **Fontana dell'Ovato★★★** The Oval Fountain is dominated by the statue of the sibyl, flanked by allegorical figures of rivers.
- **Fontana dell'Organo★★★** The Organ Fountain once played music on a hidden water-powered organ. This ingenious mechanism was invented by a Frenchman, Claude Venard, in the 16C.

Villa Gregoriana★ – *Largo Sant'Angelo. 0774 38 27 33. www.villagregoriana.it. Open Tue–Sun Apr–mid-Oct 10am–6.30pm (mid-Oct–Mar 2.30pm). Closed Dec–Feb. €5.* A tangle of steep paths winds down wooded slopes to where the Aniene plunges through a craggy ravine. Pope Gregory XVI diverted the river to ease flooding in 1831 and created the **Great Waterfall★★**, to the right down the path from the entrance. A strenuous walk brings you to a late Republic **Temple of Vesta**. Eighteen Corinthian columns still adorn the hillside, now in the garden of the Ristorante Sibilla *(0774 335 281; www.ristorantesibilla.com)*.

©Davide Romanini/Dreamstime.com

Villa d'Este, Tivoli

Castelli Romani★★

Approx 22mi/35km southeast of Rome. Take Via Tuscolana S 215 (exit 21 on Michelin map 563).

This attractive region in the Alban Hills has been the country retreat for affluent Romans for centuries. Cicero and Emperors Tiberius, Nero, and Galba had country houses here. The name, "Roman Fortresses," originated in the Middle Ages, when noble families sought refuge from the anarchy in Rome by fortifying outlying villages. The "Castelli" form a circle around the edge of an immense, long-extinct volcanic crater.

Don't miss:

*   **Frascati★** Frascati is known for its white wine and for its 16C and 17C villas, particularly the **Villa Aldobrandini★** *(visit by appointment only: contact the Ufficio del Turismo, Piazza Marconi; 1, 06 68 33 785; www.aldobrandini.it; gardens open summer Mon–Fri 9am–1pm, 3–6pm (winter 5pm); closed public holidays),* set high above terraces, clipped avenues, fountains, and rockeries.

*   **Grottaferrata** The fortress-like medieval **abbey★** is at the end of the main street. The church of **Santa Maria di Grottaferrata★** has an attractive 10C marble font, and the chapel of St Nilus has a 17C coffered ceiling and frescoes by Domenichino.

*   **Monte Cavo** *Road toll €1 per person.* Huge paving stones remain from the Sacred Way that led to the Temple of Jupiter on top of Monte Cavo. From the square there is a fine **view★**.

Nemi

G. Bludzin/MICHELIN

*   **Nemi** This village occupies a **site★★** in a natural amphitheater on the slopes of a crater now filled by Lake Nemi.

*   **Tomb of the Horatii and the Curiatii★** This late Republic monument beside the road leading into Albano is made of huge blocks of peperine.

*   **Albano Laziale** The town probably derives its name from Domitian's Villa Albana. Look out for the brick church of **Santa Maria della Rotonda★** with its bold 13C Romanesque campanile. The **Villa Communale★** is a huge public garden with vestiges of Pompey the Great's villa.

*   **Castel Gandolfo★** Famous as the pope's summer residence, this village is on the edge of the Lago di Albano. The **Papal Villa** *(closed)* was built in 1628 on the site of Domitian's 1C villa.

*   **Ardea** A detour 19mi/30km south brings you to Ardea and the **Museo della Raccolta Manzù★★** *(06 91 35 022; www. museomanzu.beniculturali.it; open Mon 2–7pm, Tue–Sun 9am–7pm; closed Jan 1, Christmas)* which holds works by the sculptor Giacomo Manzù including sculpture, drawings, engravings, and jewelry.

Lago di Bracciano★★

24mi/39km northwest of Rome

Lake Bracciano occupies a series of volcanic craters in the Sabatini Mountains, not far from Viterbo. A boat service operates on the lake, allowing visitors to explore the villages with their charming old houses and narrow alleyways.

Don't miss:

- **Anguillara-Sabazia★** Entry to this medieval town, 670ft/185m above sea level, is through an impressive 16C gate decorated with a clock. From the small square next to the 18C **Collegiate Church of the Assumption** there is a magnificent view across the lake.

- **Trevignano Romano** This characteristic medieval town extends along the lake shore. From Via Umberto I, the road rises up the hill to the **Church of the Assumption**, which has frescoes inspired by the School of Raphael.

- **Bracciano★** The main attraction of this old town is the impressive **Castello Orsini-Odescalchi★★★** *(06 99 80 43 48;*
www.odescalchi.it; open Apr–Sept Tue–Sat (Aug Mon–Sat) 10am–noon, 3–6pm (Oct–Mar 5.30pm), Sun, public holidays 9am–12.30pm; guided tour 1hr; €7). The castle was originally built around the medieval Rock of the Prefects of Vico, who governed the town until the 13C. It passed to the Orsini family in 1419. Six cylindrical towers mark the outer limits of the castle, which was built almost entirely of lava rock on top of volcanic tufa. Two walls surround the monument and the medieval township. A spiral staircase leads up to the first rooms on the main floor. Pope Sixtus fled the plague here in 1481. Inside, one of the rooms has a ceiling fresco by Taddeo Zuccari, and there is a bust of *Paolo Giordano II Orsini* by Bernini. The **Sentry Walk** connects the towers and offers a glorious panoramic view. Steps then lead down to the charming **central courtyard★** with its double doors and external staircase made of lava.

- **Museo Storico dell'Aeronautica** – *see For Kids*

Arms Room, Castello Orsini-Odescalchi

Lara Pessina/MICHELIN

EXCURSIONS

Ostia Antica★★

15mi/24km southwest of Rome. Viale dei Romagnoli 717. 06 56 35 02 15. www.archeoroma. beniculturali.it. Disabled access with assistance, and only for the museum. Museum and excavations: open Apr–Oct Tue–Sun 8.30am–1hr before dusk. Closed Jan 1, May 1, Christmas. €6.50.

The best-preserved Roman ruins outside Pompeii, the ancient port of Ostia once stood at the mouth of the Tiber, hence its name— *ostium* is the Latin word for mouth. The coastline has since retreated so now the ruins are about a mile inland. Ostia was established around the 4C BC, and flourished until the 4C, with a population reaching 100,000 at its peak. The first harbor was sited on the right bank of the river, roughly where Leonardo da Vinci Airport now is. When this became too small Hadrian built a second one inland. It was hexagonal in shape, lined with docks and warehouses, and was joined to the Tiber by a canal, the Fossa Trajana.

As Rome declined in the 4C, so too did Ostia. The harbors silted up, malaria depopulated the town, and eventually it was abandoned. Although the ruins were pillaged for building materials, the site remained buried under sand for centuries and so is remarkably well preserved. The plan of the town is easy to follow, with the main street, the Decumanus Maximus, running through the center lined with shops and public buildings. Most of the citizens lived in blocks of apartments called *insulae*, while wealthier people had private houses *(domus)*. Several places of worship dedicated to different religions have been discovered, reflecting the diverse population of a port city.

Don't miss:

♦ **Terme di Nettuno** This 2C building has a terrace with a view of the fine **mosaics★★** depicting the marriage of Neptune and Amphitrite.

♦ **Horrea di Hortensius★** These grand 1C warehouses *(horrea)* are built around a pillared courtyard and lined with shops.

♦ **Theater★** Augustus probably provided the theater, which has been much restored.

♦ **Piazzale delle Corporazioni★★★** Under the portico in the square were the offices of 70 trading corporations. Mosaic emblems show what commodity they traded.

THE TIBER DELTA IN THE 2C AND TODAY

– – – – – Coast at beginning of 20C

Leonardo da Vinci
Museo delle Navi
Porto di Claudio
Via Portuense
TEVERE
Fiumicino
Porto di Traiano
Fiumicino Fossa Traiana
ISOLA SACRA
★ **Necropoli**
Ostia Antica
Via Ostiense
S 296
SCAVI DI OSTIA ★★
Lido di Ostia
0   2 km

Mosaic flooring, Domus di Amore and Psiche

- **Casa di Diana★** A striking example of an *insula*, with rooms and passages arranged around an internal courtyard.
- **Thermopolium★★** The name means "sale of hot drinks." There's a marble counter and paintings of the produce.
- **Museum★** This contains reliefs, statues, frescoes, and a series of fine **portraits★** from the site.
- **Capitolium and Forum★★** The **Capitolium** was the largest temple in Ostia, built in the 2C and dedicated to Jupiter, Juno, and Minerva. Although the marble facing is missing from the walls, the brick remains are impressive. The **forum** was enlarged in the 2C. At the far end stands the 1C **Temple of Rome and Augustus**, a grandiose building once faced with marble. The **Terme del Foro★** were the largest baths in Ostia.
- **Casa del Larario★** This building consists of shops ranged around an internal court. The recess, decorated in attractive red and ocher bricks, housed the statues of the Lares, the protective household gods.
- **Horrea Epagathiana★** This 2C warehouse complex has a fine doorway with columns and a pediment.

- **Domus di Amore and Psiche★★** This 4C private house has mosaic and marble floors, and a *nymphaeum* decorated with niches, arcades, and columns.
- **Insulae del Serapide★** These 2C blocks have porticoes around a courtyard and a bathhouse.
- **Baths of the Seven Sages★** These feature a number of interesting mosaics.
- **Casa dei Dioscuri** Built in the 4C, the floors of this house are paved with beautiful multi-colored mosaics.
- **Terme della Marciana** Behind the massive pilasters of the frigidarium apse, a beautiful **mosaic★** shows athletes in various poses, with trophies and equipment.
- **Schola del Traiano★★** This impressive 2–3C building was the headquarters of a guild of merchants. On the left of the entrance is a copy of a statue of Trajan found here.
- **Necropolis of Trajan's Port★** *3mi/5km from the excavations. 06 56 35 80 01. http://archeo roma.beniculturali.it. Open by appointment only Mar–Oct 1st Thu and last Sat of each month 9am–6pm.* Isolated and silent, the necropolis is studded with trees. The inhabitants of Trajan's Harbor buried their dead here from the 2C–4C.
- **Museo delle Navi Romane** *Fiumicino. 06 65 01 00 89. Closed for restoration at the time of going to press.* The maritime museum is on the site of the original Claudian Harbor. It houses the hulls of five Roman vessels and smaller articles including pottery, needles, and money.

EXCURSIONS

Catacombe di Priscilla★

Ⓜ *Line B: Bologna*

This fascinating district stands outside the old walls northeast of the city. Pleasant residential streets are lined with elegant *palazzi* and dotted with the attractive gardens of patrician villas.

Don't miss:

♦ **Sant'Agnese Fuori le Mura★**
06 86 20 54 56. www.santagnese. net. Open daily 9am–1pm, 4–6pm. In the 4C Constantia, Constantine's daughter, erected a huge basilica near the tomb of the martyr St Agnes, after praying to her to be cured of leprosy. It has been much restored but retains the 4C plan. The ceiling and baldacchino are 17C. The 7C **apse mosaic★** is typical of Roman art with Byzantine influences. The **catacombs** *(06 86 10 840; guided tours only; open daily 9am–noon, 4–6pm; closed Oct 24–Nov 21, public holidays; €8)* date back to the 2C.

♦ **Mausoleo di Santa Costanza★★** *06 86 10 840. Open daily 9am–noon, 4–6pm. Closed public holidays.* Emperor Constantine's daughters, Helen and Constantia, were buried in this circular 4C mausoleum, which was probably converted into a church in the 13C. The dome rests on a drum supported by 12 pairs of granite columns. The surrounding barrel-vaulted gallery is still adorned with its original 4C **mosaic★**, which depicts floral and geometric details, portraits in medallions, and vine tendrils entwined with harvest scenes.

♦ **Catacombe di Priscilla★★**
06 86 20 62 72. Guided tours only (35min) Tue–Sun 8.30am–noon, 2.30–5pm. Closed Easter, Christmas. €8. The catacombs developed out of a private underground chamber *(hypogeum)* beneath the house of the Acilii, a noble family to which Priscilla belonged. In the 4C, St Sylvester's Basilica was built by Pope Sylvester over the graves. The **Chapel of the Taking of the Veil** is named after its fresco, thought to represent three episodes in the dead woman's life. The **Chapel of the Virgin and Child★** contains the earliest representation of the Virgin. The **Greek Chapel★** consists of two chambers.

♦ **Mosque★** *06 80 82 167. Open Wed & Sat 9–11.30am. Groups by appointment only. Closed Aug and during Ramadan.* The mosque uses typical Roman building materials to underline its connection to the city. The **interior★** is the real masterpiece; the prayer hall is surmounted by a large stepped dome and 16 side domes.

♦ **Casina delle Civette** *06 06 08. www.museivillatorlonia.it. Open Apr–Sept Tue–Sun 9am–7pm (Oct–Mar 5pm). Closed Jan 1, May 1, Aug 15, Christmas. €3.* The **House of the Owls** (as Casina delle Civette translates) is a quirky 19C building best known for its collection of Roman Liberty-style **stained-glass windows★**. It is hidden amid the green surroundings of Villa Torlonia, built at the beginning of the 19C for the wealthy banking family.

MUST SEE

EUR★

Ⓜ *Line A: EUR Fermi*

This neighborhood was conceived by the Fascist government in 1937 for a international exhibition, the "Esposizione Universale di Roma," which was to have taken place in 1942 but was abandoned because of the war. The project was given fresh impetus in the 1950s, and the suburb was completed along much the same lines as those of the original plan. The Palazzo dello Sport was designed by Nervi and Piacentini for the Rome Olympics. The marble buildings now house government offices and several museums. The suburb was intended to glorify Fascism, but in spite of the sensation of being in some kind of bombastic overplanned utopia it remains a popular place to live.

Highlights:

◆ **Museo della Civiltà Romana**★★ *06 06 08. www.museociviltaromana.it. Assisted visits are available for disabled visitors. Open Tue–Sat 9am–2pm, Sun 9am–1.30pm (last admission 30min before closing time). Closed Jan 1, May 1, Christmas. €6.50.* The huge **Museum of Roman Civilization** sprawls across two buildings linked by a portico. It illustrates the city's history from its foundation through to the Empire, and shows how a peasant people conquered the entire known world. Highlights are a large model of 5C BC Rome, called the "plastico," and a superb **scale model**★★ of Rome at the time of Constantine, made by the

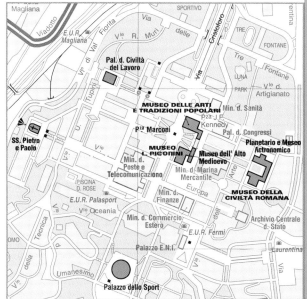

EXCURSIONS

architect Italo Gismondi in 1937. Other replicas bring to life the Colosseum, Domitian's Stadium, and Hadrian's Villa. Of particular interest is the model depicting the spiral of low-relief panels on **Trajan's Column**. There is also an planetarium.

* **Museo delle Arti e Tradizioni Popolari★** – see For Kids
* **Museo Preistorico Etnografico L. Pigorini★** 06 54 95 21. www.pigorini.arti.beniculturali. it. Open Mon–Sat 10am–6pm. Closed Jan 1, Easter Mon, Christmas. €6. The **Museum of Ethnography and Prehistory** houses one of the largest ethnographical collections in the world. The rich **African Section** assembles more than 60,000 objects, including weapons, utensils, costumes, and religious articles. The **Oceanic Section** features masks, sculptures, and paintings. The second floor is dedicated to paleontology. The last room focuses on the early Etruscan era (late 8C to mid-6C BC). The **Praenestina fibul★** bears one of the oldest inscriptions in Latin.
* **Museo dell'Alto Medioevo** Viale Lincoln 3. 06 54 22 81 99. Open Tue–Sat 9am–1.30pm, Mon & Thu 9am–7.30pm. Closed

The Square Colosseum
Built for the 1942 World Exhibition, which never took place due to World War II, Mussolini intended EUR's most iconic building, the Palazzo della Civiltà del Lavoro, to celebrate the Colosseum, and to link his regime with everything that the ancient Roman landmark represented. It is sometimes referred to as the Colosseo Quadrato (square Colosseum).

Jan 1, May 1, Christmas. €2. The **Medieval Museum** contains exhibits covering the 5C to the 11C, as well as plans of Classical and Christian Rome.

* **Palazzo della Civiltà del Lavoro** Clad in travertine marble pierced with arches, this stark palace houses administrative offices.
* **Santi Pietro e Paolo** This spectacular travertine church, dedicated to St Peter and St Paul, was built between 1937 and 1941 on the highest point in the EUR. Set among shrubs and flowers, the white building dominates the district. At the top of the steps stand large statues of St Peter and St Paul.

Palestrina★

26mi/ 42km southeast of Rome.

Palestrina is a small and attractive medieval town perched on the slopes of the Prenestini Hills, with stunning views of the surrounding countryside. According to legend, ancient Praeneste was founded at the dawn of Roman history by Telegonus, the son of Ulysses and

Palazzo della Civiltà del Lavoro

© Vose/Dreamstime.com

Nile Mosaic, Museo Archeologico Prenestino

the enchantress Circe. The town's heyday was during the 8C and 7C BC, and it was often besieged because of its important strategic position. It had become a favorite country retreat by Imperial times. The fabulous funerary ornaments found in the 8C necropolis, which are now on display at the **Museo Nazionale Etrusco di Villa Giulia** *(see Major Museums)*, reveal Palestrina's illustrious past.

Don't miss:

* **Temple of Fortuna★**

    This temple was part of a grandiose sanctuary dedicated to the goddess Fortune. Built during the 2C–1C BC, it is one of the most important examples of Roman architecture in Italy. The complex, which was abandoned in the 4C, would have occupied most of the area now covered by the town; it was made up of a series of terraces linked by a system of ramps and stairways. A large basilica-shaped room, two lateral buildings, a natural cave, and an apse paved with the famous Nile Mosaic survive from the lower sanctuary. The upper sanctuary was on the fourth terrace of the temple complex, where Piazza della Cortina is now.

* **Museo Archeologico Prenestino** *Entrance at the top of the stairs up to the Terrazza degli Emicicli. 06 95 38 100. www.archeologia.beniculturali. it/pages/atlante/S66.html. Open 9am–1hr before dusk. Closed Jan 1, May 1, Christmas. €3.* The Palazzo Colonna-Barberini, houses the archeological museum and curves dramatically around the ancient Temple of Fortune. The highlight of its collection is the late 2C BC **Nile Mosaic★★**, one of the largest and finest Hellenic mosaics, which shows the river in flood with stranded animals, hunters, and boaters among the islands. Notable also is **Il Triade Capitolina★★**, the only known depiction of Rome's three tutelary gods, Minerva, Jupiter, and Juno, all squashed onto one throne.

Town center – The main square, **Piazza Regina Margherita**, replaced the ancient forum. The 11C **church of St Agapito** was constructed among the ruins of a Roman temple. At the center of the piazza is a statue of Giovanni Pierluigi da Palestrina (1524–94), Renaissance composer of polyphonic religious music.

FOR KIDS

Rome does not have much in the way of special facilities for small children, and the lack of public toilets is a problem. However, the Italians themselves are very welcoming of children, and as long as you don't try to cram too much in there are fun things to do that kids will enjoy.

ANCIENT ROME

For many of Rome's archeological sites it can be difficult for children to imagine the original buildings from the ruins that remain. The **Colosseum** (see page 46) is an obvious exception, and few can resist stories of gladiators and wild beasts. **Trajan's Market** (see page 40) is also sufficiently well preserved that you can see quite easily what it looked like.

MUSEUMS

Rome's museums are among the finest in the world, and even if your kids groan at the very mention of the word, there are places that will capture their interest. The **Capitoline Museums** (see page 86) often run special programs for children, and the others listed here should prove popular.

Colosseum, where gladiators fought wild beasts

©Susan Smart/APA Publications

Museo degli Strumenti Musicali★

See map p 83. 06 70 14 796. www.galleriaborghese.it. Open Tue–Sun 8.30am-7.30pm. Closed Jan 1, May 1, Christmas. €4.

The charming **Museum of Musical Instruments** has everything from from antique whistles, horns, and handbells to exotic instruments such as inlaid mandolins, tambourines, ocarinas, and the 17C Barberini harp, decorated with amazing gilt carvings. Look out for the rare 17C vertical harpsichord.

Museo delle Arti e Tradizioni Popolari★

See map p 113. Piazza Marconi 8. 06 59 26 148. www.popolari. arti.beniculturali.it. Open Tue–Fri 9am–6pm, Sat, Sun and public holidays 9am–8pm. Closed Jan 1, May 1, Christmas. €4.

This beautiful museum introduces visitors to Italian folklore and traditions. Exhibits include Sicilian carriages and a Venetian gondola. Other displays explore peasant life, breadmaking, farming, hunting, salling, and fishing. There are also musical instruments, puppets, and marionettes. The **Museo della Civiltà Romana★★** (see p 113) nearby has a fantastic scale model of 4C Rome, and children will also enjoy the ethnographic collections in the **Museo Preistorico Etnografico L. Pigorini**.

Museo Explora ©Museo Explora

Museo Explora★

Via Flaminia 82. 06 36 13 776. www.mdbr.it. Visits must be pre-booked. Open Tue–Fri 9.30am–11.30am, 3–5pm, Sat and festivals 10am–noon, 3–5pm. Closed Jan 1, Aug 15, Christmas. €7.

The first Italian museum devoted to 🐾**kids** is a child-sized play-town where everything can be touched and experimented with, and it has displays on the body, the environment, communication, and society.

Museo Nazionale delle Paste Alimentari

See map p 53. Piazza Scanberbeg 117. 06 69 91 120. www.museo dellapasta.it. Open 9.30am–5.30pm. Closed public holidays. €10. Audio guide. Closed for restoration at the time of going to press.

The **National Pasta Museum** charts eight centuries in the history of Italy's national dish through an array of imaginative, informative, and amusing displays. Not far away in the Quirinale district is the tiny **Museo delle Cere** (Waxworks Museum. *Piazza S Apostoli 67; 06 67 96 482; open daily 9am–8pm; €6*).

Museo Storico dell'Aeronautica

See p 109 Aeroporto Vigna di Valle. 06 99 88 75 08. www.aeronautica. difesa.it. Open Tue–Sun 9.30am–5.30pm (winter 4.30pm). Closed Jan 1, Easter, May 1, Christmas.

The **Aerospace Museum** near Lago di Bracciano explores the history of flight through photographs, weapons, uniforms, and shiny ranks of restored airplanes.

PARKS & PLAYGROUNDS

There are a lot of green spaces within easy reach of the city center where small people can let off steam after an improving dose of culture. If you are feeling athletic, you can hire bikes and ride out into the countryside along 🐾**Via Appia Antica** *(see map p 85)* or on the cycle tracks along the Tiber to the north of the city.

Borghese Gardens

See p 102.

Rome's most famous gardens offer pony rides, a small funfair, a road train, and a boating lake. There are also bikes and rickshaws for hire. The old-fashioned zoo was disappointing, but the newer **Bioparco**

Bioparco, Borghese Gardens ©Alfredo Falcone/Dreamstime.com

is an improvement. Just next door, the pretty gardens on **Il Pincio** (see map p 77) are good for hide and seek, and you should look out for the water clock.

EUR★

See map p 113.

This district has a huge old-style amusement park, **LunEUR** (Via delle Tre Fontane; open Mon–Fri 3–8pm, Sat 3–1am, Sun 10am–1pm, 3–10pm; entrance free, charges for rides), with a Ferris wheel, ghost trains, and all kinds of rides. There is also a swimming pool to the south of the suburb, the 🏊**Piscina delle Rose** (06 54 22 03 33; www.piscinadellerose.com; open Jun–Sep, 10am–10pm Mon–Fri, 9am–7pm Sat–Sun)

Gianicolo★

See p 104.

The tree-lined road along the top of the hill offers fine views of Rome. There is a carousel near Piazzale Giuseppe Garibaldi, pony

Ferris wheel, LunEUR

©Stefano Corso/iStockphoto.com

Cooling off

When the heat becomes a bit too much, kids (and parents) can dip a toe in the open-air pool at the All'Ombra del Colosseo summer festival (see p 121). Just a few minutes from the Colosseum, you can't beat the location. Parents can keep an eye on the fun from the poolside.

rides, and balloon vendors, and a puppet show runs at weekends between 10am and 3pm.

Aquapiper

Free bus from Piazza della Repubblica. Via Maremmana Inferiore 354, Guidonia Montecelio. 07 74 32 65 38. www.aquapiper. it. Jun–Sept open daily 9am–7pm. €16, €20 Sun. One child aged 0–10 free with each paying adult.

If you want to escape the heat of the city, this aquatic park, about 15mi/25km east of Rome, is one of the largest in the region. It has swimming pools of all sizes, including shallow areas for young children to splash about in, water slides, rivers for rafting, and the biggest wave machine in Europe. There are plenty of tables, chairs, and loungers for relaxing.

Villa Doria Pamphili

See p 105.

This enormous park is a popular place for picnics, and it also has grotto-fountains and playgrounds. Beware of restrictions about playing on the grass that, however bizarre, are often enforced.

MUST DO

QUIRKY ROME

Not all of the art in Rome is serious and high-minded, and if you keep your eyes open there are artistic and architectural oddities all over the place. Here are a few examples.

Stone animals

In **Piazza della Minerva** *(see p 64)* you will find an elephant carrying an Egyptian obelisk on its back. If you are visiting the **Galleria Doria Pamphili** *(see p 91)*, see if you can spot the stone cat that gives its name to the **Via della Gatta** nearby. There are little turtles going for a dip on the **Fontana delle Tartarughe★** *(see p 101)* and bees drinking from the **Fontana delle Api** *(see p 78)*.

Architectural oddities

The **Cappuccini crypt★★** in Santa Maria della Concezione *(see p 78)* is ghoulishly decorated with thousands of skulls. In **Via Piè di Marmo** *(see map p 64)* there is a huge stone foot which is no longer attached to its owner, and a bit farther along is the **Fontana del Facchino**, whose fat porter pours water from his barrel for passersby. Check who is telling the truth with the **Bocca della Verità** in Santa Maria in Cosmedin *(see p 98)* and see if you can find the game boards that the ancient Romans marked out on the floor of the **Basilica Giulia★★** in the Roman Forum *(see p 34)*. Visit the **church of Sant'Ignazio** *(see map on p 64)* and admire the domed ceiling that isn't a dome at all.

ICE CREAM

Italian ice cream is world famous and Rome is ice cream heaven with *gelaterie* at every turn. These are just a few recommendations.
Della Palma – *Via della Maddalena 20/23, Piazza della Rotonda*. This *gelateria* has 135 different flavors.
Duse (da Giovanni) – *Via Duse1/e, zona Parioli*. In an elegant district near the Catacombe di Priscilla, this has unusual flavors like date, passion fruit, and papaya.
Il Gelato di S. Crispino – *Via Acaia 55/56, Laterano*. Considered one of the best in Rome, flavors include honey with ginger and cinnamon, liquorice, and meringue with hazelnut.
Pica – *Via della Seggiola 12, Campo dei Fiori*. Renowned for its rice and ricotta ice creams.

Il Gelato di S.Crispino

© Il Gelato di S.Crispino

FOR KIDS

119

SPORTS AND ACTIVITIES

Spectator sport in Rome is focused firmly on football, with local teams Roma and Lazio vying for supremacy. There are also tennis and golf tournaments and the Six Nations rugby competition in which Italy takes part. The Rome Marathon is held in March. If you want to play sports rather than watch there are various facilities available.

EUR★

This district (map p 113) contains a cluster of sports stadia, with the **Palazzo dello Sport**, an impressive building by architect Pier Luigi Nervi, used for basketball, and the **Velodromo**, both built for the 1960 Olympics.

Monte Mario

The city's sporting hub, the green slopes of Monte Mario provide an attractive backdrop to this district. Here you will find the **Foro Italico**, begun by the Fascist government in 1928 and the venue for most sports events in the city. The road to the Piazzale del Foro Italico is paved with

mosaics of "Il Duce." The Italian Open tennis tournament is staged here each year in May, and the Olympic swimming pool is also located here. The austere **Stadio dei Marmi** also dates to the 1930s, as does the **Stadio Olimpico**, though it was remodeled before the 1960 Olympics and several times since. The stadium is home to AS Roma and SS Lazio, who play on alternate Sundays (match tickets on the day from the stadium, 06 23 79 10, or from Lottomatica stores; €20–120). On the other side of the river is the **Stadio Flaminio** (06 45 21 31 91; www.federugby.it), where the Italian rugby union team plays, and the **Palazzetto dello Sport**.

Rome Cavalieri

ACTIVITIES

Golf

Most clubs will welcome non-members who have membership cards for their home club and proof of handicap. Try the **Circolo del Golf di Roma** *(Via dell'Acqua Santa 3; 06 78 03 407; www.golf roma.it)* and the **Golf Club Arco di Costantino** *(Via Flaminia; 06 33 62 44 40; www.golfarco.it)*.

Health clubs

These are not always open to visitors, and they can be expensive. The **Roman Sport Center** in Villa Borghese *(Viale del Galoppatoio 33; 06 32 18 096; http://www.romansportcenter.com)* and the **Freetime Sporting Club** *(Via Ussani 82; 06 65 35 901; www.freetime.org)* welcome nonmembers and offer the usual range of facilities such as swimming pools, weight rooms, squash courts, and saunas.

Running and Cycling

These are the easiest ways to counter the effects of the vacation pastries and ice cream. There is no shortage of open spaces for jogging, and you can admire the fashions of the locals as you exercise. Villa Borghese has a running track as does Villa Glori and there are lots of places around the city where you can hire bikes with which to venture farther afield.

Swimming

The **Piscina delle Rose** *(see p 118)* is popular with locals and tourists, and **Juventus nuoto** *(Via Bravetta 539; 06 66 16 09 85; open Jun–Sept 8am–6.30pm Mon–Fri)* and **Oceania Village** *(Via del Cappellaccio 20; 06 592 18 85)* are water parks with various facilities. Some hotels, such as the **Rome Cavalieri** *(Via Alberto Cadlolo 101; 06 3509 1; www.romecavalieri.it)* open their pools to nonresidents, though these can be expensive. During the **All'Ombra del Colosseo** summer festival *(end Jun–beg Sept)*, cool off near the Colosseum *(06 70 03 17 01; www.allombradelcolosseo.it)*.

Tennis

There are facilities in the **Foro Italico** *(Via delle Olimpiade; 06 36 85 41 40; www.ctforoitalico.it)* and at the **Circolo Tennis Tor Carbone** *(Via Tor Carbone 41; 06 718 34 94; www.torcarbone.it)*.

SPORTS AND ACTIVITIES

SHOPPING

Rome is a great place for shopping while sightseeing. Many of the shops are near some of the historic sites so you can combine both activities and enjoy a pleasant lunch or drink along the way. We have included some of the highlights here but you will discover your own delights. Some clothes stores close on Monday morning and food shops shut their doors on Thursday afternoon but in the historic center they remain open all day; elsewhere they are generally open from 10am–1pm and 4–7.30pm (winter) or 5–8pm (summer).

FASHION

Rome offers a range of boutiques and one-off shops. If you're looking for luxury and labels head to **Via Veneto** and the area between **Via del Corso** and **Piazza di Spagna**. Versace, Fendi, and Laura Biagiotti await your custom. If your eyes are bigger than your budget, you can windowshop till you drop in **Via del Condotti**, where Valentino, Bulgari, Dolce & Gabbana, Prada, and Armani line up along with the unmissable Louis Vuitton store. **Via del Corso** is packed with young shoppers on a Saturday afternoon and **Via Nazionale**, **Via del Tritone**, and **Via Cola di Rienzo** buzz with people-watching and shopping opportunities.

Bomba

©Bomba

Bomba – *Via dell'Oca 39/41. 06 32 03 020. www.cristinabomba.com.* This boutique sells simple, elegant designs loved by fashionistas.

Claudio Sanò – *Largo Osci 67/A. 06 44 69 284. www.claudiosano.it.* Quirky and offbeat leather bags created by a true artist.

David Saddler – *Via del Corso 103. 06 80 01 59 54. www.david-saddler.com.* English-style jackets, trousers, gloves, and shirts at reasonable prices.

Il Discount dell'Alta Moda – *Via di Gesù e Maria 14/16. 06 36 13 796.* Previous season's designs at major discounts. A second branch is in Via del Viminale 35.

Franco Borini – *Via dei Pettinari 86/87. 06 68 75670.* Outrageous footwear including vertiginous heels and acid-bright colors.

Galleria di Orditi e Trame – *Via del Teatro Valle 54/b. 06 68 93 372.* Two innovative artists create beautiful and original cotton hats for this boutique.

Maga Morgana – *Via del Governo Vecchio 27. 06 68 79 995.* Fashionistas in the know head here for knitwear, coats, and skirts.

MUST DO

ANTIQUES

Antiques collectors should take a stroll around the Piazza di Spagna district along **Via del Babuino**, home to the city's most prestigious antique dealers. Stop off at **Oasi Antiquariato** at no. 83 and then head to **Via Margutta**, brimming with art galleries and workshops in which marble and silver objects are restored. Head to **Via dei Coronari**, near Piazza Navona, for shops specializing in 19C furniture. The narrow alleyways around **Piazza Campo dei Fiori** and **Piazza Farnese** are worth investigating as well.

FOOD AND DRINK

Rome is your oyster for cheese, coffee, chocolate, meats, truffles, ice cream, and, of course, pasta. Chocaholics should head to **Said Dal 1923** chocolate factory *(Via Tiburtina 35, San Lorenzo; 06 44 69 204 www.said.it)* or **La Bottega del Cioccolato** *(Via Leonina 82, Fiori Imperiali; 06 48 21 473; www.labot tegadelcioccolato.it)*. A paradise for cheese lovers awaits at **Latticini Micocci** *(Via Collina 14, Port Pia; 06 47 41 784; www.micoccidis tribuzione.it)*. For pasta, try **Gatti e Antonelli** *(Via Nemorense 211, Catacombe di Priscilla; 06 86 21 80 44; www.gattiantonelli.it)*. Venture into deli heaven at **Volpetti** *(Via Marmorata 47, Testaccio; 06 57 42 352; www.volpetti.com)*, where you can sample wild boar ham, Piedmontese cheese with white truffles *(crutin)*, Italian caviar *(calvisius)*, infused oils, and Italian spirits. For your stylish kitchen supplies, including Alessi products, head to **c.u.c.i.n.a.** *(Via Mario dei Fiori 65)*.

BOOKSHOPS

The most famous bookshops enjoy spacious premises in central Rome, offering a wide selection of books, DVDs, and stationery. **Feltrinelli** *(www.lafeltrinelli.it)* has well-stocked bookshops throughout the city, including Via Orlando 78/81, near Piazza della Repubblica, where the whole shop is dedicated to foreign books, and **Mondadori** *(www. negozimondadori.it)* has many branches, including one near the Trevi Fountain. Other bookshops include **Mel Book Store** *(Via Nazionale 254/255)* and **Rinascita** *(Via delle Botteghe Oscure 1)*. **Bibli** at Via dei Fienaroli 28 boasts readings and literary events, and just a few doors away **Al Tempo Ritrovato** celebrates women writers. **Fahrenheit 451** *(Piazza Campo dei Fiori)* is a maze of rooms that bookworms will adore. The **Lion Bookshop** *(Via dei Greci 33)* has a wide selection of English books and a café in which to enjoy reading them.

MARKETS

For a true flavor of Roman life stroll around the markets, which offer a wide range of goods, produce, enticing smells, bright colors, and local interest. They are often noisy, busy, and lively affairs and well worth investigating for fresh food and flowers, gifts to take home, or an unexpected bargain. A perfect way to spend a few hours in the city. Try to get there early to avoid crowds.

Borgo Parioli – *Via Tirso 14, Catacombe di Priscilla. Open Sat–Sun.* This antiques market is held in a large garage and boasts a selection of paintings, prints, frames, clocks, embroidery, lace, books, and magazines. There's also a wide range of curios, but the prices can be a little on the steep side. Unusual culinary specialties may also be sampled here.

Garage Sale – Rigattieri per Hobby – *Piazza della Marina, Borghetto Flaminio 32, Villa Giulia. Open Sun.* Clothes and other items are sold at this market, which also specializes in chic secondhand goods, and antiques, as well as general bric-a-brac.

La Soffitta sotto i Portici – *Piazza Augusto Imperatore, Piazza di Spagna. Open 1st and 3rd Sun in the month. Closed Aug.* Frequented by dealers and collectors alike, this market sells paintings, prints, frames, small items of furniture, ceramics, and lace. Known for its bargains it is held in a large, rather splendid square.

Mercatino Biologico – *Via Cardinale Merry del Val, Trastevere. Open 2nd Sun in the month.* This market sells environmentally friendly produce, including organic food, recycled paper, plant-based soaps, and wooden toys.

Mercatino di Ponte Milvio – *Piazzale di Ponte Milvio. Open 1st weekend in the month, Sat afternoon, Sun all day.* This market under Milvio Bridge sells a panoply of furniture, craftwork, and art.

Mercato dell'Antiquariato di Fontanella Borghese – *Piazza Borghese, Piazza di Spagna. Open Mon–Sat mornings.* An excellent market for those interested in old books and prints.

Mercato dell'Antiquariato di Piazza Verdi – *Piazza Verdi, Villa Borghese. Open 4th Sun in the month.* As well as antiques and arts and crafts, this market also sells amphorae, old friezes, and coats of arms. There is also a wide selection of books for children.

Mercato delle Stampe – *Largo della Fontanella di Borghese. Open Mon–Sat mornings.* If you still love the printed word in all its forms in this digital era, then this is the market for you. Like an outdoor library, it's bursting with old prints, books of various conditions and values, and specialist magazines. It's a good spot to snap up an antiquarian or art book but you will need to hone your bargaining skills first.

Mercato di Campo dei Fiori – *Campo dei Fiori. Open Mon–Sat mornings.* The oldest in

Rome, there has been a market on this spot for around 140 years. It sells the best fish in the city, fruit and vegetables, and spices, as well as household goods, toys, and gorgeous cheap floral bouquets.

Mercato di Piazza San Cosimato – *Piazza S. Cosimato, Trastevere. Open Mon–Sat mornings.* One of the busiest markets in central Rome, it is divided into two sections: the *fruttaroli* stallholders buy their produce every morning from the wholesale market, and the *vignaroli* sell produce grown in their own gardens.

Mercato di Piazza Vittorio Emanuele – *Via Lamarmora, Santa Maria Maggiore. Open mornings, daily.* Once held on the huge square, the market has moved to an indoor site nearby. One of the cheapest markets in Rome, it is renowned for its fresh fish, its excellent selection of cheeses, and Oriental spices.

Mercato di Testaccio – *Piazza di Testaccio. Open Mon–Sat mornings.* Nicknamed "*er core de Roma*," (the heart of Rome), this market has a wide selection of goods, including leather shoes at factory prices.

Mercato di Via Sannio – *Via Sannio, S. Giovanni in Laterano. Open Mon–Sat mornings.* A wide choice of reasonably priced new and secondhand clothes, as well as stalls selling leather shoes at factory prices.

Porta Portese – *Via Portuense, Trastevere. Open Sun mornings.* Selling a little of everything, this is the main flea market in Rome. It opened officially during World War II. Articles for sale include general bric-a-brac, new and secondhand clothes, photographic equipment, books, and CDs. You will need to try out your haggling skills, but don't expect to get a real bargain. Beware of pickpockets.

Underground – *Via Crispi, Parcheggio Ludovisi 96, Piazza di Spagna. Open 1st weekend of the month, Sat afternoons, Sun all day.* This flea market held in a huge underground car park has a variety of antiques, collectors' items, modern articles, and costume jewelry. Spend a few hours browsing.

Porta Portese market

MARKETS

NIGHTLIFE

Nightlife in Rome is varied, lively, and often noisy. Bars, clubs, and music venues abound. If you enjoy a glass of wine outside on a balmy evening or a romantic stroll over the Tiber, there are plenty of bars waiting to be discovered in the district between Piazza Campo dei Fiori and Piazza Navona. Head to Trastevere if you are looking for live music and to Testaccio and Ostiense for the city's most popular nightclubs. The locals know how to party and tend to do so relatively late. They like to meet at a bar first and then head for dinner at around 9pm. Wine bars stay open until midnight (or beyond in the summer), and for Romans, the biggest clubbing nights are Friday and Saturday. Smart casual is the dress code in this city.

STAGE & SCREEN

Tickets for most events can be bought online at www.listicket.it.

Theaters

Casa dei Teatri

Large 3 Giugno 1849 (corner of Via di S. Pancrazio). 06 45 44 07 07. www.casadeiteatri.culturaroma.it. Closed Mon.

An innovative spin on theater, the recently founded Casa dei Teatri, located in the Villino Corsini in Villa Pamphili, looks at performance from all angles, and combines its productions with research, training courses, and workshops.

Teatro Argentina

Largo Argentina 52. 06 68 80 46 01/2. Box office: closed Mon.

Built at the beginning of the 18C, this large theater staged the first performance of the *Barber of Seville* in 1816. It enjoys an excellent location opposite the Roman ruins of Largo Argentina, and offers a program mainly of drama.

Teatro Quirino

Via Marco Minghetti 1, Fontana di Treve. 06 67 94 585. www.teatro quirino.it. Box office: closed Mon.

The theater focuses on traditional drama, although experimental plays are occasionally staged here.

Teatro Valle

Via del Teatro Valle 21, Piazza Navona. 06 68 80 37 94. www.teatro valle.it. Box office: closed Mon.

This magnificent 18C building, located near Piazza Sant' Eustachio, hosts performances of many of the Italian classics. Sadly, the theater is threatened with closure.

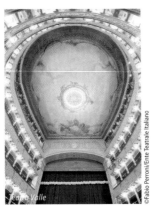

Teatro Valle

©Fabio Perroni/Ente Teatrale Italiano

MUST DO

Classical, opera, and ballet

Venues range from traditional theaters, usually in the old center, to modern venues staging more contemporary shows, often located near the university. A whole range of musical events can be booked through **Il Sogno – Gente e Paesi** (*Via Adda 111; 06 85 30 17 55*).

Auditorium dell'Accademia Nazionale di Santa Cecilia

Via della Conciliazione 4, Vaticano. 06 80 82 058. www.santacecilia.it.

This prestigious concert hall is the setting for concerts by some of the best-known orchestras and conductors from across the globe.

Auditorium Parco della Musica

Viale Pietro di Coubertin. 06 80 24 12 81. www.auditorium.com.

A fabulous multipurpose music complex designed by Renzo Piano. Located in the northern suburbs it has three large concert halls and a fourth, open-air venue constructed in the style of Greek and Roman theaters. There's a wide range of events to suit all tastes.

Teatro dell'Opera

Piazza Beniamino Gigli 1, Santa Maria Maggiore. 06 48 16 01 255. www.opera.roma.it. Tickets can be purchased up to 1hr prior to shows. Online booking: www.amitsrl.it.

Recommended for fans of classical music, opera, and ballet, this large theater provides subtitles for shows in foreign languages. In summer the venue moves to Caracalla's Baths (*see panel*)

Summer venues

The Teatro dell'Opera moves to the Baths of Caracalla for the summer opera and ballet season. A wonderful venue and cast: Pavarotti, Domingo, and Carreras have all performed here (*Termi di Caracalla, Valle delle Terme di Caracalla; www.opera.roma.it*). Classical concerts are also held in the beautiful gardens of the 16C Villa Giulia in the summer (*Piazzale di Villa Giulia; 06 39734576*).

Teatro Olimpico

Piazza Gentile da Fabriano 17, Monte Mario. 06 32 65 991. www.teatroolimpico.it. Box office: open 11am–1pm, 3–7pm, and 8–9pm on the day of performance.

This theater on the banks of the Tiber is the headquarters of the Accademia Filarmonica Romana. Broadway musicals, ballet, and some comic opera are staged here.

Teatro Sistina

Via Sistina 129, Piazza di Spagna. 06 42 00 711. www.ilsistina.com.

Renowned for its excellent acoustics, this theater hosts famous musicals, as well as concerts by acclaimed international performers.

Cinemas

Rome has plenty of cinemas, several of which show English language movies daily. Check the listings magazines or websites (not all have English versions) for the latest information. Movies in English will have the letters "VO" (*Versione Originale*) next to them, but do check their original language is English and not German or Spanish, for example. Other films are generally dubbed into Italian and so are only suitable for those who speak the language. Some cinemas don't allow latecomers, so make sure you arrive in good time.

In addition to the arthouse cinemas and multiplexes, Rome has small clubs, such as **Filmstudio**, which may require a membership card *(Via degli Orti d'Alibert 1/c, Trastevere; www.filmstudioroma. com)*. However, the cards are either free or very cheap, much like social clubs *(centri sociali, see p 132)*. Cinemas typically screen at 4.30, 6.30, 8.30, and 10.30pm. Paying by credit card is still rare at movie theaters, so be prepared to pay in cash.

Alcazar

Via Merry del Val 14, Trastevere. 06 58 80 099.

Traditional-style cinema screening VO films on Mondays.

Casa del Cinema

Largo Marcello Mastroianni 1, in Villa Borghese, enter from the Piazzale del Brasile. 06 42 36 01. www.casadelcinema.it.

Multisala Barberini

G. Bludzin/MICHELIN

In the wonderful setting of the grounds of Villa Borghese, this state-of-the-art complex shows a wide range of VO films, including arthouse, videos, and free documentaries. You can watch a DVD at one of the computers and there's a good café. A film festival is held here in October.

Cinecittà

Via Tuscolana 1055. 06 72 29 31. www.cinecittastudios.it.

A large movie studio in the southern suburbs where *Ben Hur* and *Cleopatra* were made, and where films and TV shows (including an episode of *Dr Who*) are still made. Only guided tours for media and school groups are possible at the time of going to press. A cinema theme park is under consideration.

Metropolitan

Via del Corso 7, near Piazza del Popolo. 06 32 00 933. www.mymovies.it.

In a conveniently central location, this cinema shows VO films on a regular basis.

Multisala Barbarini

Piazza Barberini 24/25/26. 06 48 27 707. www.multisalabarberini.it.

Multiscreen venue showing all the latest Hollywood blockbusters, plus some interesting Italian offerings.

Quirinetta

Via Marco Minghetti 4, near Via del Corso. 06 67 90 012.

There are regular screenings of VO films in this cinema with a central location. No entry if you are late!

Warner Village

Moderno, Piazza della Repubblica 45. Call center 89 211 (no prefix), www.thespacecinema.it.

Large, modern, multiscreen venue located just next to Repubblica metro showing VO films daily. Check the website to see what's on. The program usually changes on Fridays.

Open-air cinemas

During July and August, the open-air "villages" set up during the Estate Romana festival offer cinema-lovers the chance to see a number of films. Check out www.cineporto.com for the latest screenings at **Cineporto** *(Via Antonino di san Giuliano, Ponte Milvio, near the Olympic Stadium)* and **Isola del Cinema** *(Isola Tiberina between the Ponte Cestio and Ponte Fabricio; 06 58 33 31 13; www.isoladel cinema.com; open Jul–Sept).*
At the **Nuovo Sacher**, owned by Italian film legend Nanni Moretti, a projector is set up outside in the summer. VO films are screened on Mondays and there is a bar and bookshop on site too *(Largo Ascianghi 1, Trastevere; 06 58 18 116; www.sacherfilm.eu).*

CLUBS & BARS

Jazz clubs

Rome is a big player on the jazz scene and there are a number of great clubs and venues.

Alexanderplatz
Jazz & Image festival

Via Ostia 9, Vaticano-San Pietro. 06 39 74 21 71. www.alexander platz.it. Closed Sun and Jul–Aug.

Some of the greatest jazz musicians

Film festivals
The **International Rome Film Festival** is held in late October *(www.romacinemafest.org)* and the **Roma Independent Film Festival** in March or April *(Via Po 134; 06 45 425 050; www.riff. it)*. In autumn, the city hosts the **Cinecittà Internet Film Festival** *(www.cinecittastudios.com).*

in the world have played here, with concerts starting at 10.30pm. The Alexanderplatz Jazz Image festival is held in June and July in the Villa Celimontana park *(www.celimontanajazz.com).*

Big Mama

Vicolo S. Francesco a Ripa 18, Trastevere. 06 58 12 551. www.bigmama.it. Closed Mon.

Brick walls and huge names: this club has international jazz and blues appeal.

Casa del Jazz

Viale di Porta Ardeatina 55. 06 70 47 31. www.casajazz.it.

There's room for 150 fans at this great jazz complex in the southern suburbs. There is also a café and a restaurant. Local and international musicians, some established, others on their way to stardom.

La Palma Jazz Club

Via Giuseppe Mirri 35. 33 95 27 50 19. www.lapalmaclub.it

Try not to miss La Palma, one of Rome's best jazz clubs with an outdoor courtyard and restaurant. It also hosts jazz festivals.

NIGHTLIFE

Bars

Antico Café della Pace

Via della Pace 5, Piazza Navona. 06 68 61 216.

This atmospheric spot has been here since the late 18C and is full of paintings from the period. Favorite haunt of artists, politicians, and chic locals. See and be seen.

Casa Bleve

Via del Teatro Valle 48/4, Pantheon. 06 68 65 970. www.casableve.it.

A fabulous and elegant wine bar. Not cheap but a wonderful experience and delicious food to match the selection. Good buffet lunch.

Doppiozeroo

Via Ostiense 68. 06 57 30 19 61. www.doppiozeroo.it.

This sleek upmarket wine bar attracts a young and trendy crowd. Come for coffee the morning after to recover from the night before…

Freni e Frizioni

Via del Politeama. Trastevere. 06 45 49 74 99. www.freniefrizioni.com.

Bohemian, arty, and hip, ex-mechanics workshop that is now a cool cocktail joint, on the banks of the Tiber overlooking the lovely Piazza Politeama. Serves good drinks, buffet-style food, and a bucketful of atmosphere.

Il Nolano

Piazza Campo dei Fiori 11, Campo dei Fiori. 06 68 79 344.

Atmospheric, slightly bohemian, and arty wine bar—a good option if it's too busy or noisy at La Vineria. It takes its name from Giordano Bruno da Nola, whose statue you can see from here.

Jonathan's Angels

Via della Fossa 16, Piazza Navona. 06 68 93 426.

It's often difficult to find a seat in this popular piano bar, which is deliberately kitsch and decorated with paintings by the owner. You can also enjoy the eccentricity of Rome's most famous toilet, complete with statuary.

La Vineria Reggio

Piazza Campo dei Fiori 15, Campo dei Fiori. 06 68 80 32 68.

Everybody in Rome knows "Vineria." It was one of the city's first wine bars and the locals meet

Freni e Frizioni

©Freni e Frizioni

here for pre- and post-dinner drinks. You may have to fight for a table, but if you want atmosphere, conversation, and reasonably priced wines, then give it a try.

Lancelot

Via dei Volsci 77/a. 06 44 54 675.

This bar is particularly popular with students and has over 300 board games available to customers. It boasts a good beer and cocktail list, in addition to a reasonable selection of light meals, filled rolls and salads.

Le Coppelle 52

Piazza del Coppelle 52 (off Via delle Coppelle), Pantheon. 06 68 32 410.

Lounge on the eccentric armchairs outside and enjoy a ginger mojito in this fabulous open-air bar. Great atmosphere.

The Library

Vicolo della Cancelleria 7. 06 45 49 58 11. www.thelibrary.it.

A recent addition to this gentrifying neighborhood, this bar designed along feng shui principles targets an international crowd. Owner Dana serves a light menu and provides wifi. Live music and DJ on Fridays and Saturdays.

ORVM, The Westin Excelsior

Via Vittorio Veneto 141, Via Veneto. 06 47 081.

Stylish venue in a smart hotel decorated in elegant Art Deco style where locals meet for cocktails before heading out to dinner. Don't miss Happy Hour (in fact two hours!), which starts at 6.30pm

Palatium Enoteca Regionale

Via Frattina, Centro Storico. 06 69 20 21 32. www.enotecapalatium.it.

This is in a great location near the Spanish Steps and popular with professionals at lunchtime and then at Happy Hour. An *enoteca* that specializes in wines and food from the Lazio region. Stylish, minimalist, atmospheric.

Salotto 42

Via di Pietra Papa 42, Pantheon. 06 67 85 804. www.salotti42.it.

Hip, chic but with a relaxed ambience, this cocktail bar boasts a marriage of Swedish and Roman style (and a smorgasbord on a Sunday). It has an extensive library of books on fashion, art, and design. Think while you drink.

Clubs

In the mood for clubbing? Head to **Via di Monte Testaccio** and the nearby streets, where you'll find venues for all ages and tastes. We have included a variety of clubs in different locations, so once you find your (dancing) feet you can venture farther afield. Ostiense has some hip bars and a few *ristodiscos*, where you can both eat and dance. Opening days and times vary so check the listing magazines. Admission varies from no charge to €15.

Akab-Cave

Via di Monte Testaccio 69, Piramide Cestia–Testaccio. 06 57 25 05 85. www.akabcave.com. Closed Sun.

Great concerts followed by disco with funk and soul, and good cocktails. A popular spot for locals—some big names have performed here. Check the website to see who the next A-lister will be.

Alibi

Via di Monte Testaccio 44. 06 57 43 448. www.lalibi.it. Open Thu–Sun 11pm–5am.

One of the city's original gay clubs but now attracting a more mixed crowd, who enjoy the great roof terrace. Mostly house and disco.

Alpheus

Via del Commercio 36, Piramide Cestia-Testaccio. 06 57 47 826. Closed Mon and Aug. www.alpheus.it.

One of the district's many clubs, located in an old warehouse. You can enjoy concerts and cabarets and there are three dance floors.

Anima

57 Via Santa Maria dell'Anima, Centro Storico. 06 68 64 021. Open daily 9pm–4am.

The place for funk, soul, reggae and house enjoyed with a cocktail. Hip venue with unusual interior and stylish clientele.

Caruso Café de Oriente

Via di Monte Testaccio 64. 06 57 45 019. www.carusocafe.com.

Cuban and Latin American music, followed by DJs at this atmospheric spot. Salsa the night away.

Distillerie Clandestine

Via Giuseppe Libetta 13, Ostiense. 06 57 30 51 02. www.distillerie clandestine.com.

This *ristodisco* has an elegant retro style. Resident DJs play house, electronica, and hip-hop.

Drunken Ship

Campo dei Fiori 20. 06 68 30 05 35. Open daily until 2am. www.drunkenship.com.

Italy's original and most famous American club-bar. The atmosphere is welcoming and the club is in a perfect location. DJs are on hand most evenings and there's a Happy Hour.

Centri Sociali

If you want to feel the real pulse of the live music scene in Rome, investigate the Centri Sociali, non-profit social centers that were once underground but are now almost mainstream. They operate in "appropriated" community spaces, holding concerts, plays, film screenings, and dance events, and tickets are cheap. One of the most popular is in north Rome: **Brancaleone** *(Via Levanna 11; 06 82 00 43 82; www.brancaleone.it)* features Italian and international DJs, a cinema club, and art exhibitions.

The Estate Romana Festival

During the summer, most nightclubs move out to cooler premises along the exclusive Fregene Beach. A number of open-air concerts are held in the various "villages" within the capital, where books, CDs, and clothes—as well as snacks and drinks—can be bought, before dancing the night away or grabbing a table and listening to the music. The most famous of these include **Testaccio Village**, which welcomes a number of international artists every year; the **Foro Italico**, where annual cabaret shows are held; **Parco di Villa Celimontana**, for jazz concerts; **Parco di Villa Ada Savoia**, for new sounds; and for Latin-American music, the **Fiesta** (www.estateromana.comune.roma.it).

Goa Club

Via Giuseppe Libetta 13, Ostiense. 06 57 48 277. Open Tue–Sat 11pm–4am.

Very popular, trendy, large disco playing hip house, and techno-electro, with excellent DJs. Central bar with sofas. Closed most Sundays except for last in the month when a women-only event is held.

Il Locale

Vicolo del Fico 3, Piazza Navona. 06 68 79 075. Closed Mon.

Il Locale is divided into a number of simply furnished rooms. It's a good place in which to see Italian rock groups.

Jackie O

Via Boncompagni 11, Centro Storico. 06 42 88 54 57. Open Tue–Sun, until 4am.

If you're looking for glitz, glitter, and glamor then head to Jackie O. A popular venue for affluent locals and visitors. Enjoy drinks at the piano bar before hitting the dance floor and then the restaurant. Good live music too and a chance to join in with Italian and English songs.

Micca

Via Pietro Micca 7. 06 87 44 00 79. www.miccaclub.com. Closed in summer.

Located in an immense underground space, Micca's program ranges from themed nights (including toga parties, of course) to guest DJs and burlesque shows.

Piper

Via Tagliamento 9, Catacombe di Priscilla. 06 85 55 398. www.midra.it. Closed Mon–Wed.

Opened in 1965, this famous nightclub now organizes themed evenings, including rock, underground, and 1970s music.

Micca

©Ursula Persiani/Micca Club

NIGHTLIFE

RESTAURANTS

Long a proponent of Slow Food—local recipes and fresh, indigenous ingredients—the Eternal City's eateries shine, from the humblest pizzeria or trattoria to the temples of haute cuisine. Venues listed below were selected for their ambience, location and/or value for money. Rates indicate the average cost of an appetizer, an entrée and a dessert for one person (not including tax, gratuity or beverages). Call for information regarding reservations, dress code and opening hours. In Rome, lunch *(pranzo)* runs from 12.30–3pm and dinner *(cena)* goes from 8–11pm; restaurants generally close around midnight. Avoid the tourist menus *(menu turistico)* as the food is often inferior.

| Inexpensive | € | under €25 | Expensive | €€€ | €50–70 |
| Moderate | €€ | €25–50 | Luxury | €€€€ | over €70 |

Aventino/ Piramide Cestia– Testaccio

Da Oio a Casa Mia

€ **Roman**
Via Galvani 43–5, Testaccio. 📞 *06 57 82 680. Closed Sun and Aug.*

Brick arches soar over red-checked tables in this neighborhood trattoria. The menu concentrates on Roman offal—like tripe and a scramble of heart, liver, spleen and lung with artichokes or onions. Vegetarians will no doubt prefer the chickpea soup or meatless pasta dishes like tagliolini *cacio e pepe* (broad pasta with sheep's cheese and pepper).

Pizzeria Ad

€ **Pizza**
Via G. Bove 43, Piramide Cestia– Testaccio. 📞 *06 57 46 372. Closed Mon, mid- to late-Aug, end of Dec.*

Deep-dish pizzas here appeal to those who enjoy the Neapolitan thick-crust pies. Despite the spacious dining room and the seating that sprawls outdoors in summer, there is never an empty table here.

Estro Bar

€€ **Italian**
Abitart Hotel, Via Pellegrino Matteucci 20, Ostiense. 📞 *06 572 89 141. www.estrobar.com.*

This trendy eatery does triple duty: as a pizzeria, gallery and wine bar in the hip outpost of the Abitart Hotel (www.abitarthotel.com), which almost single-handedly is gentrifying Ostiense. Truffle lasagnetta with lobster, shrimp and artichokes makes a good *primi*, before digging into a hearty Chianina beef stew with polenta gratin.

Tuttifrutti

€€ **Italian**
Via Luca della Robbia 5, Testaccio. 📞 *06 57 57 902. Closed Mon, school holidays and Aug. Booking recommended.*

This restaurant is run by a cultural association that employs young artists. The cuisine is simple, yet original, and the daily changing menu includes a list of appetizing antipasti. The sweet dessert wine and chocolate are produced by Trappist monks.

MUST EAT

Checchino dal 1887

€€€ **Roman**
Via Monte Testaccio 30, Testaccio.
℘06 57 46 318. www.checchino-
dal-1887.com. Closed Sun–Mon,
Dec 24–Jan 2, Aug. Booking
recommended.

This restaurant specializes in butchers' off-cuts—oxtail, offal and tripe—as befits its location across from the old slaughterhouse. Specialities include oxtail, rigatoni alla *pajata* (fasting calf intestine), and sweetbreads in white wine sauce. Less expensive meals of cheese and vegetables are available at lunchtime.

Catacombe Di Priscilla (Via Nomentana, Via Salaria)

La Mora

€ **Tuscan**
Piazza Crati 13, Catacombe di
Priscilla. ℘06 862 06 613.
www.ristorante-lamora.it. Closed
Mon and Aug; no lunch Wed.

This friendly, informal restaurant specializes in Tuscan cuisine and wood-fired pizzas. For steak-lovers, there's a delicious *bistecca alla Fiorentina* made with beef raised in the Chiana Valley. Desserts, such as panna cotta and torta della nonna, are made in-house.

Colosseo–Celio/Fori Imperiali/Piazza Venezia/Rione Monti

Enoteca Al Vino Al Vino

€ **Sicilian**
Via dei Serpenti 19, Monti.
℘06 48 58 03. Closed last three
weeks in Aug.

This charming wine bar boasts colorful ceramic tables, friendly service and a lively atmosphere. Then there's the excellent selection of wine from all over Italy. Try the assortment of cooked meats and cheeses (the saltiest of which are served with honey) and delicious Sicilian specialities like the homemade caponata.

Hasakura

€€ **Japanese**
Via dei Serpenti 27, Monti. ℘06 48
36 48. Closed Sun, Aug, and four
days at Christmas.

This simply furnished Japanese restaurant is noted for its fresh ingredients and excellent sushi. The trendy address offers better value for money at lunchtime.

Eur

La Taverna del Porto

€€ **Roman**
Via Cristoforo Colombo 551,
EUR. ℘06 54 21 01 81/77.
www.latavernadelporto.com.

A rustic-style Roman restaurant with a hearty traditional menu that is based firmly on meat and wine. You'll feel right at home in the friendly and warm atmosphere

Fontana di Trevi–Quirinale

Pizzeria Est Est Est

€ **Pizza**
Via Genova 32, Quirinale. ℘06 48
81 107. Closed Mon and Aug.

This family-owned place is one of the oldest pizzerias in Rome, and its Art Nouveau décor dates from the early 20C (look for the small cherub pouring the so-called "mayor's water"). Don't leave without sampling the restaurant's namesake sweet white wine, made in northern Lazio.

Il Giardino di Albinot

€€ **Sardinian**
Via Zucchelli 29, Trevi. ℘ 06 48 85 202. www.ilgiardinodialbino.it.

The family that runs this casual and friendly place offers typical Sardinian cuisine. Both the fish and meat dishes are excellent.

Isola Tiberina– Torre Argentina

Enoteca La Bottega del Vino da Anacleto Bleve

€ **Italian**
Via S. Maria del Pianto 9/A, Largo Argentina. ℘ 06 68 65 970. Closed evenings and public holidays.

This wine bar lies in the heart of the Jewish quarter. Before taking a seat, choose from the delicate soufflés, roulades, salads and cheeses displayed at the bar. For a sweet finish, try the delicious lemon or coffee gelato.

Quelli della Taverna

€ **Roman**
Via dei Barbieri 25, Torre Argentina. ℘ 06 68 69 660. www.renatoeluisa.it. Closed Mon, Aug, and 24–26 Dec. Booking recommended.

Run by two friends, this cozy taverna serves drinks and traditional pasta dishes in terra-cotta crockery, as it was presented in days gone by. Be sure to try the fabulous focaccia.

Al Pompiere

€€ **Roman**
Via S. Maria de' Calderari 38, Torre Argentina. ℘ 06 68 68 377. www.alpompiereroma.com. Closed Sun and Jul 15–Aug 30.

Enjoy a range of traditional Roman-Jewish dishes served in the spacious rooms of an old palazzo. The homemade *crostata di ricotta e visciole* (ricotta and sour cherry tart) is worth the caloric splurge.

Sora Lella

€€ **Roman**
Via di Ponte Quattro Capi 16, Isola Tiberina. ℘ 06 68 61 601. www.soralella.com. Closed Sun, Easter, Aug, Dec 24–26, and Jan 1.

This famous restaurant was once run by Lella Fabrizi, the sister of actor Aldo. It is now managed by her son, who has extended the traditional range of family recipes to include new specialities. Don't miss the *formaggi alle marmellate* (cheese with sweet fruit jelly) and the desserts.

Monte Mario

Osteria dell'Angelo

€ **Roman**
Via G. Bettolo 24, Monte Mario. ℘ 06 37 29 470. Closed Sun and public holidays. Lunch on Tue and Fri only.

This lively trattoria, decorated with rugby shirts (all the waiters wear one), serves traditional Roman dishes, including tonnarelli *cacio e pepe*, rigatoni *con pajata*, *coda alla vaccinara* and *trippa alla Romana* (♨ *See Typical Roman Cuisine.*) The fixed-price dinner menu on offer is good value.

La Pergola

€€€€   **Italian**

Via Cadolo 101, Hotel Cavalieri Hilton, Monte Mario. ☏ 06 35 092 152. www.romecavalieri.com. Closed Sun and Aug 8–23.

Set atop Monte Mario, this famous restaurant—with its 53,000-bottle wine cellar—is one of Rome's best. German chef Heinz Beck creates modern Italian fare like grilled lobster on aubergine caviar, and tangerine risotto with scampi carpaccio and mint. There's a free shuttle bus from the city center.

Pantheon/Montecitorio

L'Eau Vive

€   **French**

Via Monterone 85, Pantheon. ☏ 06 68 80 10 95. www.restaurant-eauvive.it. Closed Sun and Aug. Booking recommended.

"Living Water"—located inside the 16C Palazzo Lante—is run by missionary nuns from around the world. Sample the restaurant's French specialities and international dishes in the large, frescoed dining room on the first floor.

Vecchia Locanda

€   **Italian**

Vicolo Simibaldi 2, Pantheon. ☏ 06 68 80 28 31. www.vecchialocanda. eu. Closed Sun and Dec 22–Jan 22. Booking recommended.

In a narrow street between Largo Argentina and the Pantheon, this small, elegant restaurant is known for its beef and fresh homemade pasta. The atmosphere resembles a Roman inn, with tables set outside in the summer.

Grano

€€   **Italian & Mediterranean**

Piazza Rondanini 53, Pantheon. Open daily noon–midnight. ☏ 06 68 19 20 96. www.ristorantegrano.it.

Whether you prefer to sit outside at the small outdoor tables or inside to admire the many artistic elements (the restaurant was designed by cartoonist Enzo Apicella), you will savor the rich menu of Mediterranean and classic home-cooked Italian food.

Osteria dell'Ingegno

€€€   **Italian**

Piazza di Pietra 45, Montecitorio. ☏ 06 67 80 662. Closed Sun and two weeks in Aug. Booking required.

This charming bistro in the shadow of Hadrian's Temple is always crowded at lunchtime. The menu includes elaborate dishes that are flavored with aromatic herbs, as well as a wide selection of charcuterie and cheeses.

La Rosetta

€€€€   **Seafood**

Via della Rosetta 9, Pantheon. ☏ 06 68 61 002. www.larosetta. com. Closed Sun lunchtime and Aug 8–22. Booking recommended.

When La Rosetta was established in 1966, it was Rome's only seafood restaurant. Fish and shellfish are delivered fresh every morning and evening to chef Massimo Riccioli's kitchen, where they star in such à la carte dishes such as risotto with clams, sweet onion cream and coriander; Catalana-style lobster millefeuille; and wild sea bass in lemon sauce with crispy prawns and asparagus.

Piazza Navona/ Campo Dei Fiori/ Castel Sant'Angelo

Enoteca L'Angolo Divino

€ **Italian**
Via dei Balestrari 12, Campo dei Fiori. 06 68 64 413. Closed Sun lunchtime and Mon evening.

This old wine and oil store has been converted into a rustic, simply furnished wine bar, lined with bottle-filled shelves. While you sip a glass of wine at the bar, you can enjoy tarts, roulades and homemade pasta dishes.

Da Francesco

€ **Roman**
Piazza del Fico 29, Piazza Navona. 06 68 64 009. Closed Tue lunchtime.

The attractive Piazza del Fico is home to this lively trattoria, which serves typical Roman dishes, including pizzas, an excellent focaccia with dry-cured ham, as well as various types of pasta. All this and a cheerful atmosphere.

Osteria Ar Galletto

€ **Roman**
Piazza Farnese 102, Vicolo del Gallo 1, Campo dei Fiori. 06 68 61 714. Closed Sun.

This Piazza Farnese restaurant was founded in 1484 and was once known as the Osteria dei Borgia. Roasted chicken is the signature dish (*galletto* means "little rooster"), and there is a wide choice of sauces for pasta. Ham is still cut by hand in front of customers here.

Pizzeria Da Baffetto

€ **Pizza**
Via del Governo Vecchio 114, Piazza Navona. 06 68 61 617. www.pizzeriabaffetto.it. Closed Sun (except in summer) and Aug.

"Summer of Love" radicals made this place trendy—now everyone jostles for a seat at this straightforward establishment. The pizzas are crisp and can be topped with everything from speck (a type of prosciutto) to spinach. Service is brusque in classic Roman style.

Da Tonino

€ **Italian**
Via del Governo Vecchio 18, Piazza Navona. 33 35 87 0779. Open daily except Sun.

Only open in the evening. This trattoria, too small even for a sign, often asks customers to share tables in the congenial atmosphere. Mop up delicious pasta and meat sauces from your plate with some homemade bread.

Enoteca Al Bric

€€ **Italian**
Via del Pellegrino 51, Campo dei Fiori. 06 68 79 533. www.albric.it. Closed for two weeks in Aug. Booking recommended.

This popular bistro offers a wide choice of wines—more than 1,000 labels—around which to design your meal. Cheeses and charcuterie come from several countries, with an emphasis on France. Similarly, Calvados and Armagnac feature on the cocktail list together with bitters and Grappa.

Grotto del Teatro di Pompeo

€€ **Italian**

Via del Biscione, Campo dei Fiori.
✆ 06 68 80 36 86. Closed Mon.

Dine near the site of Julius Caesar's assassination. A palazzo gradually barnacled the ruins of the Theater of Pompey. The chef has an impressive way with seafood— a specialty here—as well as with radicchio, the maroon chicory-like plant so beloved by Italians.

Il Drappo

€€ **Sardinian**

Vicolo del Malpasso 9, Piazza Navona. ✆ 06 68 77 365.
www.ildrappo.it. Closed Sun and Aug. Booking recommended.

Traditional Sardinian specialities made from prime-quality ingredients take center stage in this quiet and friendly restaurant, where the walls are decorated with draped curtains and mirrors. Close-set tables are dressed in white linen and illuminated by candles.

Pierluigi

€€€€ **Italian**

Piazza dé Ricci 144, Campo dei Fiori.
✆ 06 68 61 302. www.pierluigi.it.
Closed Mon and 13–22 Aug.
Booking recommended.

Set in one of the most pleasant squares in Rome, this restaurant, open since 1938, has an intimate ambience whether you choose the outdoor or indoor tables. The menu focuses on seafood. Start, perhaps, with a dish of mussels sauteéd in garlic, olive oil and parsley; then move on to the salt-baked bream. Pasta dishes are equally delicious, as are the likes of a ricotta cheesecake for dessert. Impeccable service and the piazza setting add to the experience.

Piazza Del Popolo/ Piazza Di Spagna

Gina

€€ **Italian**

Via San Sebastianello 7/A, Piazza di Spagna. ✆ 06 67 80 251.
www.ginaroma.com.

This minimalist white-on-white restaurant is perfect for a quick bite or a relaxed meal. Pasta, panini and light fare make up the menu. For dessert, try the homemade crostata or the creamy gelati. Gina also provides hampers for picnickers in the nearby Villa Borghese.

La Penna d'Oca

€€ **Italian**

Via della Penna 53, Piazza del Popolo. ✆ 06 32 02 898. Closed Sun, Sat lunch, for 10 days in Jan and 20 days in Aug. Booking recommended.

This charming restaurant serves traditional cuisine, innovative seafood dishes (try the conch pie served with red onion), homemade bread, and soufflés for dessert. In the summer, you can dine on the pleasant veranda.

La Terrazza dell'Eden

€€€€ **Italian**

Via Ludovisi 49, Piazza di Spagna.
✆ 06 478 121. www.edenroma.com.
Booking recommended.

The roof garden of the Hotel Eden is home to this elegant restaurant, which offers stunning views of the city and is popular with celebrities. The creative cuisine served here centers around seafood recipes such as green-olive-crusted oven-baked sole and sea bass carpaccio. Prices for Sunday brunch are more affordable.

Porta Pia–Termini

Er Buchetto

€ **Italian**
Via del Viminale 2F, Termini. ℘06 48 83 031. Closed Sat night and Sun.

A stuffed pig guards the interior of this carvery, which has specialized in porchetta since 1890. This rosticceria is an old-school experience with just three wooden tables. Roasted pork is served in sandwiches or carved in slices accompanied by crusty rolls. Pair your meal with Castelli wines.

Pizzeria Al Forno della Soffitta

€ **Pizza**
Via dei Villini 1E/1F, Porta Pia. ℘06 44 04 642. Closed Sun.

Genuine thick-crust Neapolitan pizza is the name of the game in this no-frills pizza restaurant near the Piazza Fiume. All the ingredients come from the Campania region, and the pies are served on a round, wooden board.

Trimani il Wine Bar

€ **Italian**
Via Cernaia 37/B, Porta Pia. ℘06 44 69 630. www.trimani.com. Closed Sun, holidays and mid- to late-Aug.

This bar, run by one of the oldest families in the Roman wine business, offers an impressive selection of wines, as well as fine cuisine. The second floor provides the perfect romantic spot to sip wine; while in summer, the outdoor tables are the place to sit.

San Lorenzo Fuori Le Mura

Il Pulcino Ballerino

€ **Mediterranean**
Via degli Equi 66/68, San Lorenzo Fuori le Mura. ℘06 49 41 255. www.pulcinoballerino.com. Closed Sat lunchtime, Sun and holidays.

Founded by two childhood friends, this pleasant and informal trattoria sports stucco walls and arched entryways. They have hit on an original formula for Rome: customers can cook their own vegetables, meat, fish or cheese on a heated stone placed in the middle of the table.

Il Dito e la Luna

€€ **Sicilian**
Via dei Sabelli 51, San Lorenzo Fuori le Mura. ℘06 49 40 726. Dinner only. Closed Sun. Book ahead.

This restaurant has a pleasant bistro atmosphere. Theme evenings are occasionally held here, when Sicilian recipes, such as fish cous cous and the house signature *caponata* (Mediterranean vegetables served cold in a sweet-sour sauce), are paired with fine wines.

Santa Maria Maggiore/San Giovanni in Laterano

Pizzeria La Gallina Bianca

€ **Pizza**
Via A. Rosmini 9, Santa Maria Maggiore. ℘06 47 43 777.

Red-and-white checked tablecloths enhance the country ambience inside this popular rustic-style pizzeria, whose name means "white hen." In addition to good pizza, they also serve excellent *fritti* (deep-fried specialities). Indulge in homemade desserts, including a delicious twist on traditional tiramisu—this one is made with strawberries.

Charly's Saucière

€€ **French**
Via di San Giovanni in Laterano 270, San Giovanni in Laterano. ℘06 70 49 56 66. Closed Sat and Mon lunchtimes, Sun and Aug 5–20. Booking recommended.

Renowned as one of Rome's genuinely French eateries, Charly's has an old-fashioned, welcoming ambience. Traditional Gallic meat and fish dishes predominate, in addition to some Swiss specialities.

Agata e Romeo

€€€ **Roman**
Via Carlo Alberto 45, Santa Maria Maggiore. ℘06 44 66 115. www.agataeromeo.it. Closed Sat–Sun. Booking recommended.

Sophisticated versions of Rome's *cucina povera* star in this elegant establishment. The menu shifts with the seasons but might include saffron risotto, oxtail stew, duck cannelloni and breaded lamb chops. The *baccalà* (salted cod) is especially popular, as is Romeo's astute wine list. Chef Agata is also a cooking instructor, cookbook author and an expert on local oils and vinegars. Don't miss the excellent desserts, including the signature millefeuille.

Trastevere/Gianicolo

Pizzeria Panattoni

€ **Pizza**
Viale Trastevere 53, Trastevere. ℘06 58 00 919. Closed Wed and three weeks in Aug.

Huge marble counters earn this classic pizzeria two nicknames: *Ai Marmi* ("the marbles") and the less-appetizing *l'Obitorio* ("the mortuary"). Despite the monikers—and the cranky service—customers still flock to this pizzeria. Waiters slam down large, crispy pizzas, chilled Peroni beer and a serviceable house red wine, scowling at celebrities and "nobodies" alike.

Pizzeria Dar Poeta

€ **Pizza**
Vicolo del Bologna 45, Trastevere. ℘06 58 80 516. Closed Mon.

The line is well worth the wait at this pizzeria. Expect quirky combinations (apples and Grand Marnier) and pizzas dripping with cheese atop slow-risen crusts. The bill may be scrawled on the tablecloth, but the atmosphere is jovial and the food extraordinary.

Enoteca Ferrara

€€ **Italian**
Via del Moro 1A, Piazza Trilussa 41A, Trastevere. ℘06 58 33 3920. www.enotecaferrara.it.

Nibble at the bar, or book a table to spend the evening sampling wines from the Enoteca's main draw: its well-selected 850-bottle international list. Beyond wine, the kitchen turns out carefully prepared dishes such as perch with red cabbage and *involtini di pesce spada* (swordfish fillets rolled around cinnamon-spiked filling).

Jaipur

€€ **Indian**

Via San Francisco Ripa 56, Trastevere. Closed Mon lunch. ☎06 58 03 992. www.ristorantejaipur.it.

Rome's best Indian restaurant serves North Indian specialities from a clay tandoori oven. Spice lovers should exaggerate their normal preferences: Italians prefer ethnic food far more mild than most foreigners.

La Paella 2

€€ **Spanish**

Vicolo della Luce 3–4, near the Ponte Cestio, Trastevere. ☎06 58 33 1179. www.lapaella2.com. Closed Wed lunchtime.

Savor sangria and paella near the Tiber River. Authentic paella permutations here include fish, meat, vegetarian, lobster, shrimp, and squid ink. Paella pans and murals on the walls, red-and-white checked tablecloths and exposed-brick arches complete the rustic look of this endearing eatery.

Thai Inn

€€ **Thai**

Via Federico Ozanam 94, Gianicolo. ☎06 58 20 3145. Closed Mon and Aug.

From Piazza Venezia, take bus 44, which stops across from the Inn, just before Via Nadina Helbig. The Thai chefs here would stand out in any city—and an opportunity to sample their excellent food is certainly worth the bus trip. Christmas lights, blue lanterns, aquariums,

bamboo matting, and fake flowers and butterflies create a tranquil atmosphere.

Antico Arco

€€€ **Italian**

Via San Pancrazio 1, Piazzale Aurelio, Gianicolo. ☎06 58 15 274. www.anticoarco.it. Closed Sun and Aug.

Internationally acclaimed contemporary Italian cuisine stars inside this vine-swathed restaurant, which occupies a 19C palazzo. Picture yourself in this regal setting, dining on the likes of octopus salad; crispy suckling pig in a sweet-and-sour sauce; risotto with scorpion fish and asparagus; and homemade molten chocolate soufflé cake with vanilla and rum gelato. The wine cellar contains some 1,200 labels.

Vaticano–San Pietro

Al Limone

€ **Italian**

Viale Angelico 64/66, Vaticano. ☎06 37 22 003. Closed Sat lunchtime and Sun.

Lemons are the focal point for this restaurant, both in the restaurant's sunny decor and its tasty cuisine. Innovative regional fare, grilled entrées and homemade bread steal the show here.

Taverna Angelica

€€ **Italian**

Piazza Amerigo Capponi 6. ☎06 68 74 514. www.tavernaangelica.it. Closed for lunch, except Sun. Booking recommended.

Rustic fare with a modern twist is delivered with flair in this cozy restaurant, tucked away in the Borgo Pio district near St Peter's Basilica. The modestly sized menu lists pasta, seafood and selected meats, and there's a comprehensive Italian wine list to complement every dish. If you don't care for dolci, a list of Italian cheeses can be paired with marmalades, sauces and honey.

Venerina

€€ **Roman**
Borgo Pio 38. ✆ 06 68 64 551. www.ristorantevenerina.it.

Pasta and risotto dishes feature largely on the menu of this recently refurbished family-run restaurant, just steps away from the Vatican walls. Choose from traditional Roman cooking or international fare, both cooked to order using local produce in season. Tables on the cobbled streets outside provide entertainment as you watch the world go by.

Via Veneto

Sans Souci

€€€ **French and Italian**
Via Sicilia 20/24, Via Veneto. ✆ 06 8551 379. www.sanssouci.it. Dinner only. Closed Mon and Aug 10–20. Booking recommended.

True to its name, this well-established restaurant will melt your cares away as you dine below coffered ceilings while soft guitar music sets a romantic mood. Sans Souci's menu blends Italian and French cuisine, and recipes show off the chef's creativity. The elegant decor recalls the golden age of the Dolce Vita period; and the service is excellent.

Villa Borghese– Villa Giulia

Al Ceppo

€€ **Italian**
Via Panama 2, Villa Borghese. ✆ 06 84 19 696. www.ristorantealceppo. it. Closed Mon and Aug 8–24. Booking recommended.

This restaurant in the smart Parioli district has a rustic, yet elegant, feel. Inventive cuisine uses seasonal produce and relies on traditional recipes. Desserts include chestnut gelato with hot chocolate sauce.

Papa Guilio

€€€ **Mediterranean**
Via Giulia 14, Campo dei Fiori. ✆ 06 68 19 2650. www.ristorante papagiulio.com. Closed Tue. Booking recommended.

Dusky mirrors and leather banquettes grace this local favourite. Crisp linens, candles and crystal set the stage for innovative dishes such as pork roast in myrtle sauce. Summer invites outdoor dining in the pleasant garden.

Sapori del Lord Byron

€€€€ **Italian**
Via Guiseppe de Notaris 5. ✆ 06 32 20 404. www.lordbyron hotel.com. Closed Sun. Booking recommended.

Set in the Hotel Lord Byron in the exclusive Parioli district, this Art Deco restaurant serves perfectly executed and artfully presented regional dishes. The award-winning wine cellar includes big-name Italian and international wines, as well as some from small local wine producers.

HOTELS

From modest *pensioni* to luxury hotels, Rome has a wide range of accommodations, although finding value for money can sometimes prove difficult. Visitors should book well in advance as the capital is popular throughout the year. Generally speaking, the low season includes January, the first half of February, the last two weeks of July, the months of August and November, and the first two weeks of December. During these periods many hotels offer reasonable rates and special weekend or short break deals. Choose a hotel with air-conditioning during the summer, as it is particularly hot during this period. Breakfast may be an additional charge—and there may be an additional fee for towels in more modest establishments. The hotels listed have been chosen for their value for money, level of comfort and character. Rates quoted reflect the cost of a double room in high season.

Inexpensive	€	under €60	Expensive	€€€	€90–130
Moderate	€€	€60–90	Luxury	€€€€	over €130

For all Budgets – Hotels in this guide are grouped according to district and price (for categories see the Legend above).

Lodgings marked by the symbol € include campsites, youth hostels and modest but decent hotels, and *pensioni* with double rooms. A greater choice of charming and comfortable hotels with better quality restaurants is marked by the symbols €€ and €€€. For those in search of a truly memorable stay, the symbol €€€€ includes hotels and B&Bs with luxurious atmospheres and amenities.

Selecting a District – A good selection of *pensioni* and hotels can be found in the **historic center**, where the high concentration of tourist sights make it particularly popular. However, that popularity means that these establishments fill up quickly. The attractive quarter of **Trastevere** boasts a lively nightlife, although accommodations here are somewhat limited. Quieter and cheaper, the **Vatican and Prati**

districts are near the center. The choice around **Via Cavour** (near Monti), between Termini Station and the Fori Imperiali, is good for mid-range hotels. Many of the cheaper *pensioni* and smaller hotels are located around **Termini Station**, away from the center but well served by public transportation. You'll find Rome's luxury hotels on the **Via Veneto** and near **Villa Borghese**.

Aventino/Piramide Cestia–Testaccio

Hotel Santa Prisca

€€€   **50 rooms**
Largo M. Gelsomini 25, Aventine.
℘06 57 41 917. www.hotelsanta prisca.it.

Palms, pines and flowers wreathe this pleasant hotel on the flanks of the Aventine Hill, behind the Colosseum and less than ten minutes from the Vatican. The rooms—formerly nuns' cells—are like cameos: small, but finely wrought. All have air-conditioning, satellite TV, private baths and Internet access. A pleasant outdoor terrace at the foot of Aventine Hill provides an ideal place to watch the Roman sunsets.

Sant'Anselmo

€€€   **45 rooms**
Piazza Sant'Anselmo 2, Aventine. ☎06 570 0547. www.aventino-hotels.com. ⌨.

Swags of marble, faded gilt mirrors and citrus trees lend a Belle Epoque air to this lovely retreat, nestled high on the green-swathed hill. Rooms, all with individual names—such as *Mille baci* ("a thousand kisses") and *Camera delle poesie* ("room of poems")—boast an old-world elegance. Some have ornately draped and canopied four-poster beds, others boast intricate iron headboards.

Catacombe Di Priscilla (Via Nomentana, Via Salaria)

Hotel Santa Costanza

€€€   **74 rooms**
Viale 21 Aprile 4, Via Nomentana. ☎06 86 00 602. www.santacostanzahotel.com. ♿⌨

Comfortable, colorful armchairs fill the lobby of this hotel, which has good public transportation connections to the city center. The breakfast room, done in floral designs, has large windows looking out on an internal garden. Well-appointed rooms at this family-friendly hotel provide all the comforts of home. Parking is available for a fee.

Colosseo–Celio/ Fori Imperiali/Piazza Venezia/Rione Monti

Hotel Sandy

€   **24 rooms**
Via Cavour 136 (5th floor, no lift), Fori Imperiali. ☎06 48 84 585. www.sandyhostel.com.

Close to the Colosseum and the Roman Forum, this hostel is very popular with international visitors and young people. Spacious, colorful rooms can be shared by three to five people, with a communal bathroom (private rooms are also available). Breakfast is not served on-site, and the hostel does not accept credit cards or traveler's check.

Antica Locanda

€€   **15 rooms**
Via del Boschetto 84. ☎06 48 48 94 www.antica-locanda.com. ⌨

Located near both the Trevi Fountain and Piazza Navona, this intimate hotel couldn't be better situated. All of the en suite rooms are air-conditioned and sport a clean, neutral decor that still retains some character. Double-glazed windows ensure a good night's rest, despite being in the center of the city. The hotel also has an on-site pizzeria and a great rooftop terrace on which to enjoy a continental breakfast or a drink.

Hotel Borromeo

€€€   **30 rooms**
Via Cavour117, Colosseo. ☎06 48 5856. www.hotelborromeo.com. ♿

A five-minute walk from the Colosseum, you'll find this quiet, comfortable hotel. Recently renovated rooms sport cheery colors and picture-frame moldings. Larger junior suites offer separate living and sleeping spaces. All rooms come with Wi-Fi access, mini bars and safes; breakfast can be served in the rooms or on the rooftop terrace. Ask the helpful reception staff for area information, from good places to eat to booking tours.

Hotel Perugia

€€€ **13 rooms**
Via del Colosseo 7, Colosseo. ☎06 67 97 200. www.hperugia.it. ☎

Given its excellent location close to the Colosseum, this small four-story hotel is very reasonably priced (but has no lift). Air-conditioned rooms are simply furnished, and include thoughtful amenities such as a safe and hairdryer. One fourth-floor room has a small balcony with views of the amphitheater. The staff can help you book tickets for city tours, theater performances and sporting events.

Hotel Solis Invictus

€€€ **16 rooms**
Via Cavour 311, Fori Imperiali. ☎06 69 92 05 87. www.hotelsolis.it. ♿☎

This small, comfortable hotel is family run and is on the first floor of a building adjacent to the Roman Forum. Rooms sport sunny colors, mini bars and tiled baths; the large rooms are the most modern. Wi-Fi Internet access is available throughout the property (at a fee), and the front desk is manned 24 hours a day for guests' convenience and security.

Hotel Celio

€€€€ **18 rooms**
Via dei Santi Quattro 35/C, Colosseo. ☎06 70 49 5333. www.hotelcelio.com. ☎

Splendid fragments of frescoes add a touch of originality to rooms—all of which are named after celebrated Italian artists—in this elegant family hotel. Housed in an 1870 mansion with mosaic tile floors, the Celio also has a suite with a view of the Colosseum. Upper-floor rooms are equipped with jacuzzi tubs. Guests can eat breakfast in their room or on the terrace.

Fontana di Trevi–Quirinale

Hotel Fontana

€€€ **25 rooms**
Piazza di Trevi 96, Fontana di Trevi. ☎06 67 91 056. www.hotelfontana -trevi.com. ☎

Admire the Trevi Fountain without having to fight through the crowds at this centrally located hotel, lodged in a 14C monastery. Individually decorated rooms capture traditional style with their dark wood furnishings. Have some breakfast, afternoon tea or cocktails at the rooftop lounge and drink in the view of Rome's most famous fountain.

Isola Tiberina–Torre Argentina

Hotel Arenula

€€€ **50 rooms**
Via Santa Maria de' Calderari 47 (1st floor, no lift), Torre Argentina. ☎06 68 79 454. www.hotel arenula.com. ☎

This delightful hotel occupies a 20C palazzo in the Jewish quarter. Though basic, the natural light-filled rooms, their gray tile floors brightened by colorful curtains and bedspreads, are all equipped with private bathrooms, air-conditioning and hair dryers.

Pensione Barrett

€€€   **20 rooms**
Largo Torre Argentina 47, Torre Argentina district. ℘*06 68 68 481. www.pensione-barrett.com.* ☕€6.

This well-situated *pensione* takes its name from poet Elizabeth Barrett Browning, who stayed here for a period in 1848. Rooms incorporate thoughtful and unusual touches, such as a small footbath and tea- and coffee-making facilities; some even retain the original chestnut wood beamed ceilings. Windows are soundproofed, but for true peace and quiet, best avoid the accommodations overlooking the boisterous square.

Monte Mario

Ostello Foro Italico A.F. Pessina

€   **334 beds**
Viale delle Olimpiadi 61, Monte Mario district. (From Termini Station, Metro A to Ottaviano, then bus 32, seven stops.) ℘*06 32 36 267. www.hostels.com.* ♿☕

Just steps from the Olympic Stadium, this modern building surrounded by gardens is Rome's largest hostel—and a member of Hostelling International. Amenities include a self-service restaurant and a bar. Dorm accommodations only include six-bed rooms for men and ten-bed rooms for women. Closed midnight to 7am.

Pantheon/Montecitorio

Hotel Coronet

€€   **13 rooms**
Piazza Grazioli 5, Pantheon. ℘*06 69 92 27 05. www.hotel coronet.com.* ☕
In the 17C Palazzo Doria Pamphili, this small hotel is meticulously cared for and offers spacious, comfortable rooms, which face an interior court-yard. All the standard services apply, and the helpful staff are happy to provide information about the city, including arranging area tours.

Hotel Mimosa

€€   **11 rooms**
Via Santa Chiara 61 (2nd floor, no lift), Pantheon. ℘*06 68 80 17 53. www.hotelmimosa.net.* ☕

On the second floor of a historic palazzo, Hotel Mimosa offers good value accommodation. The lodging's main attraction is its excellent location behind the Pantheon, close to Santa Maria sopra Minerva and Piazza Navona. Well-maintained rooms are simply decorated and quiet, and small pets are welcome.

Albergo Santa Chiara

€€€€   **96 rooms**
Via Santa Chiara 21, Pantheon. ℘*06 68 72 979. www.albergo-santachiara.com.* ☕

Facing Piazza della Minerva, the Santa Chiara sits right behind the Pantheon—a great base from which to explore the Holy City. The Corteggiani family has run this lovely property since it opened in the early 1800s. Their hospitality today includes a welcoming lounge area, a bar and well-appointed guest rooms.

HOTELS

Albergo del Sole al Pantheon

€€€€   **25 rooms**

*Piazza della Rotunda 63, Pantheon.
✆06 67 80 441. www.hotelsoleal-
pantheon.com.* ⌨

One of the world's oldest hotels, this establishment traces its roots to 1467. Elegant and aristocratic, this hotel overlooks the ancient Roman temple and the lively square it anchors. Each room is individually decorated and some rooms have beautiful views of the Pantheon. Your day starts here with a rich buffet in the breakfast room, which is attached to a lovely garden patio. Jean-Paul Sartre and Simone de Beauvoir both favored this lodging.

Hotel Portoghesi

€€€€   **27 rooms**

*Via dei Portoghesi 1, Montecitorio.
✆06 68 64 231. www.hotelporto
ghesiroma.com.* ♿⌨

Opposite the legendary "Torre della Scimmia" (Monkey Tower), this hotel has pleasant rooms decorated with antique furniture and featuring flat-screen TVs and complimentary Wi-Fi access. Rooms vary in size from a small single to a superior suite with a private terrace, and a family-friendly ground-floor apartment that accommodates five guests. The glass conservatory, used as the breakfast room, and the terrace, with its views over Rome, are especially delightful.

Piazza Navona/ Campo Dei Fiori/ Castel Sant'Angelo

Hotel Navona

€€   **30 rooms**
*Via dei Sediari 8 (1st floor, no lift),
Piazza Navona district. ✆06 68*

64 203. www.hotelnavona.com. ⌨
This delightful hotel has cool, attractive rooms. The hotel is located in a 16C palazzo that was built on top of the 1C BC Baths of Agrippa. Rooms, tastefully furnished with antiques, vary in size and shape. Throughout the property, vestiges of the building's history reveal themselves in frescoes and the original exposed brickwork. Breakfast and Wi-Fi access are complimentary of the house.

Hotel Due Torri

€€€€   **26 rooms**

*Vicolo del Leonetto 23,
Piazza Navona. ✆06 68 76 983.
www.hoteldue torriroma.com.* ⌨

One of the best addresses in Rome, Hotel Due Torri was once the home of cardinals and bishops. This brick-colored residence stands slightly north of the Piazza Navona. Each room boasts its own unique decor and is furnished with a parquet floor and high-quality furniture, including some genuine antiques. "Double rooms" (two adjoining rooms with a bath in between them) suit families traveling with children.

Hotel Teatro di Pompeo

€€€€   **13 rooms**

*Largo del Pallaro 8, Campo dei
Fiori. ✆06 68 30 01 70. www.hotel
teatrodipompeo.it.* ⌨

A boutique hotel now nestles in a medieval palazzo, once the Theater of Pompey—the site of Caesar's assassination in 44BC. The pleasant hotel rooms are spacious and simply furnished. Wood-beamed ceilings and tiled floors preserve the hotel's historic charm, while private baths and air-conditioning add a modern touch.

Piazza Del Popolo/ Piazza Di Spagna

Pensione Panda

€€ **20 rooms**
*Via della Croce 35, Piazza di Spagna.
☎ 06 67 80 179. www.hotelpanda.it.*

This well-kept *pensione* in a 19C palazzo not far from the Spanish Steps has quiet, simply furnished rooms, some with a shared bathroom. Although lacking in overall charm—but offering the requisite amenities—Pensione Panda is recommended for its great location and reasonable rates.

Hotel Centrale

€€€ **21 rooms**
*Via Laurina 34, Piazza del Popolo.
☎ 06 87 40 30 890. www.hotel centraleroma.it.* ⌦

An 18C palazzo lends its space to the Hotel Centrale, now furnished in classic 19C style. Rooms offer complimentary high-speed Internet access and LCD TVs, but if it's a view you are after, book the junior suite which has a private pergola-shaded terrace with a table and deck chairs.

Hotel Condotti

€€€ **16 rooms**
*Via Mario De'Fiori 37, Piazza di Spagna. ☎ 06 67 74 661.
www.hotelcondotti.com.*

Just around the corner from the Spanish Steps and near to the fashionable boutiques on Via Condotti, the hotel greets guests in its lovely lobby, adorned with marble floors, antique furnishings, and a Venetian glass chandelier. Rooms are spread over four floors; additional accommodations are available nearby in two townhouses (breakfast included).

Hotel Parlemento

€€€ **23 rooms**
*Via delle Convertite 5, Piazza di Spagna. ☎ 06 69 92 10 00.
www.hotelparlamento.it.* ⌦

High ceilings and airy, spacious rooms decorated with plants provide this family-operated hotel with a pleasant, relaxing atmosphere. Air-conditioning is also available (at a fee). In summer, breakfast is served on an attractive terrace facing Piazza San Silvestro. Ask the concierge for help with restaurant reservations and booking area tours.

Hotel d'Inghilterra

€€€€ **88 rooms**
Via Bocca di Leone 14, Piazza di Spagna. ☎ 06 69 98 11. http://hotel dinghilterra.warwickhotels.com.

Located in the old guest-quarters of Palazzo Torlonia, Hotel d'Inghilterra has retained the elegance and charm of a 15C residence. Furnishings of the period, valuable artwork, Chinese porcelain, and fine fabrics recall the hotel's prestigious past; marble baths add even more luxury. Overlooking the fashionable boutiques along Via Borgogna, the hotel's elegant **Café Romano** is the perfect place to take a short break from shopping or to enjoy a leisurely dinner.

Hotel de Russie

€€€€ **122 rooms**
*Via del Babuino 9. ☎ 06 32 88 81.
www.russiehotel.com.*

This A-list hotel is popular with visiting stars and other prominent fig-

149

ures, who favor its sleek, trendy style. Rooms are smaller than you might expect, but full of all modern conveniences. After your treatment at the top-notch health spa—complete with a hydro pool, a Turkish steam bath, a jacuzzi, and a full fitness facility—savor an alfresco meal at the **Le Jardin de Russie**, overlooking the hotel's terraced gardens.

Porta Pia–Termini

The Beehive

€   **8 rooms**
Via Marghera 8, Termini. ✆ *06 44 704 553. www.the-beehive.com.*

Run by an American couple, this "hotel and art space" is an aesthetic, yet affordable, haven. Contemporary and minimalist in style, the Beehive uses ecologically friendly cleaning products including handmade vegetable soaps. Rooms (six doubles, one triple, and one dorm that sleeps eight) are reasonably priced, but come without TVs and air-conditioning. Free Wi-Fi is available though in the hotel's reading lounge. Three independent apartments are also available off-site.

Hotel Cervia

€€   **28 rooms**
Via Palestro 55. ✆ *06 49 10 57. www.hotelcerviaroma.com.*

This comfortable one-star hotel is just a three-minute walk from Stazione Termini—convenient if you're arriving by train. Managed by the same family since 1959, Hotel Cervia retains a friendly and homely ambience. Rooms either share bathrooms or are en suite; if you book the latter, breakfast is included in the rate. Small pets are welcome.

Hotel Tizi

€€   **25 rooms**
Via Collina 48 (1st floor, lift), Porta Pia. ✆ *06 48 20 128. www.hoteltizi.it.* ⌨ *€7.*

The hotel is named after the owner's daughter, Tiziana, who is usually on hand at the reception desk to welcome guests. Quiet, attractive rooms come both with and without bathrooms. There are not many on-site amenities or frills here, but the modest Tizi nonetheless represents good value—in a good location—for budget-minded travelers.

St. Regis Grand Hotel

€€€€ **161 rooms**
Via Vittorio Emanuele Orlando 3. ✆ *06 47 091. www.thestregis grandrome.com.*

Plush luxury with a slightly theatrical air about it reigns at the St. Regis, thanks to an unapologetic mix of Roman Empire, Regency and Louis XV styles. The hotel recently underwent a major restoration. Rooms are generous in size, with lovely appointments. In the sumptuous suites, guests have access to 24-hour butler service. The glorious lobby is a glamorous confection of potted palms and glittering chandeliers—and it is a great spot for people-watching. KamiSpa and fitness center and **Vivendo** restaurant are two more reasons to stay here.

Santa Maria Maggiore/ San Giovanni in Laterano

YWCA

€   **70 beds**
Via Cesare Balbo 4, Santa Maria Maggiore. ✆ *06 48 80 460.*

www.ywca-ucdg.it. ⌨

Accommodations here are available to women, couples and groups (not single men) in simple, clean rooms. Many of the rooms, both with and without private bathrooms, are rented out by the year to students. Amenities include a breakfast room and kitchen on the second floor, and a TV lounge on the ground floor. Closed midnight to 7am.

Hotel Piccadilly

€€   **55 rooms**
Via Magna Grecia 122,
San Giovanni in Laterano.
℘06 70 47 48 58.
www.book.bestwestern.it. ⌨

This modern hotel extends over eight floors, with the upper one serving as a light-filled breakfast venue with panoramic views of the city. Standard amenities apply in the refurbished rooms, in addition to LCD TVs and free Wi-Fi Internet access. Nearby, guests will find the Basilica of St John Lateran and the market at Via Sannio.

Hotel Mecenate Palace

€€€€   **72 rooms**
Via Carlo Alberto 3, Santa Maria
Maggiore. ℘06 44 61 354.
www.mecenatepalace.com. ⌨

Named for the Emperor Augustus' political advisor (who once lived in the vicinity), this handsome hotel occupies two 19C palaces facing the Basilica of Santa Maria Maggiore. Guests can relax in soundproofed rooms, majestically decorated in soft pastels. Happy hour on the rooftop Terrazza dei Papi, taking in the sights of Rome, is a wonderful way to wind down after a busy day.

Trastevere

Antico Borgo di Trastavere

€€   **12 rooms**
Vicolo del Buco 7, Trastevere.
℘06 58 83 774. www.trastevere
house.it. ⌨

Surrounded by restaurants and wine bars, the modest 18C palace displays exposed beams, French windows, wooden shutters and flowerpots on the balconies. All rooms have a private bath, color television and air-conditioning. Expect some late-night noise in this trendy area.

Casa di Santa Francesca

€€€   **37 rooms**
Via dei Vascellari 61, Trastevere.
℘06 58 12 125. www.sfromana.it.

Saint Francesca Romana lived in this house in the 15C, during which time she performed a host of miracles here. Today the house offers good value for quiet and peaceful simply-furnished rooms, many with small balconies and views of the Trastevere neighborhood below. The pleasant landscaped courtyard makes a good spot to relax after a day of sightseeing.

Ripa Hotel

€€€   **170 rooms**
Via degli Orti di Trastevere 1,
Trastevere. ℘06 58 611.
www.ripahotel.com.

Self-conscious minimalism rules the decor here. The lobby resembles a contemporary art exhibit with its scarlet and purple pouffes. Stark white characterizes the rooms, which are accented with splashes of black and red; most of the junior suites have terraces. For business travelers, the hotel offers meeting facilities, and there's a cafe/lounge on-site. Downstairs, DJs spin tunes in the club named **Suite**.

Vaticano–San Pietro

Colors

€ **21 rooms**
Via Boezio 31, Vatican. ℘06 68 74 030. www.colorshotel.com.

Choose between hotel or hostel rooms at this modern property. All rooms have been given a recent facelift; colorful hotel rooms include a buffet breakfast in the rate, while guests in the hostel rooms have access to free linens and a small pantry *(breakfast is available to hostel guests for P7)*. Polished floors reflect swaths of bright paint and Italian contemporary flair. A terrace surveys the skyline in this quiet quarter just north of the Vatican. Colors is a 15-minute walk from the Metro line A stop Ottaviano-San Pietro.

Hotel Alimandi Vaticano

€€€€ **24 rooms**
Viale Vaticano 99, Vatican. ℘06 39 74 5562. www.alimandivaticano hotel.com. ♿

This addition to the group of Alimandi family-owned hotels opened its doors in 2004. Marble floors, warm woods and gold tones deck the comfortable rooms out in style. In-room safe-deposit boxes are big enough to store a laptop, and all rooms have a well-stocked mini bar. You can't beat the location near the Vatican Museums, or the great amenities—such as a gym, a piano bar, and a free shuttle service to the airport.

Hotel Atlante Star

€€€€ **85 rooms**
Via Vitelleschi 34, Vatican. ℘06 68 73 233. www.atlante hotels.com. ☐

Cheerful, elegantly appointed rooms fill this hotel, which is located just two blocks from St Peter's Basilica. Deluxe rooms and suites have the best views, as well as oversized jacuzzi tubs. **Les Etoiles**, the rooftop restaurant, is aptly named, as you can dine here under the stars at night. In the summer, you can take breakfast on the rooftop terrac and take advantage of the splendid view of the Basilica.

Via Veneto

Hotel Invictus

€€ **13 rooms**
Via Quintino Sella 15, Via Veneto district. ℘06 42 01 15 61. www.hotelinvictus.com. ☐

Recently spiffed up with new fabrics in shades of blue and rose, rooms in this well-maintained hotel are pleasant and comfortable with good-quality furnishings. The property, set in the northern part of the city center, makes a fine location for those wishing to experience the "Dolce Vita" ambience, but with a modern twist—Wi-Fi available (at a fee) in all the rooms.

Villa Borghese– Villa Giulia

Hotel Villa Glori

€€€ **52 rooms**
Viale de Vignola 28, Stadio Falminio. www.villa gloriroma.com. ♿ ☐

Set in an exclusive residential neighborhood on the banks of the Tiber River, the Villa Glori enjoys a peaceful location on a tree-lined street. Refurbished rooms are homely and bright, with an emphasis on comfort. The Flaminio rugby stadium is a five-minute walk away; and with a tram stop just steps away too, all the sights of Rome lie within easy reach.

Aldrovandi Palace Hotel

€€€€　**108 rooms**
Via Ulisse Aldrovandi 15, Villa Borghese. ✆ 06 32 23 993. www.aldrovandi.com. ⌇ ⌇ €22.

This prestigious hotel just a few steps from the Villa Borghese in one of Rome's upscale residential areas boasts lovely lobby lounges furnished with antiques and magnificent crystal chandeliers. Rooms spell elegance with soft tones, marble baths and park views. Innovative Italian cuisine brings diners back to **Baby**, the Aldrovandi's acclaimed poolside restaurant.

Hotel Lord Byron

€€€€　**32 rooms**
Via Giuseppe de Notaris 5, Villa Giulia. ✆ 06 32 20 404. www.lordbyronhotel.com. ⌇

Villa Borghese gardens form the view from this small, refined hotel, whose attractive 1920s decor and peaceful atmosphere constitute a lovely respite from the bustle of the city. Plush rooms may be a little on the small side, but thoughtful extras such as towel heaters, walk-in-closets and marble bathrooms more than make up for any lack of

size. Save time to dine on fine Italian cuisine at the hotel's **Sapori del Lord Byron** restaurant.

Campsites

Flaminio Village Camping

€　　**90 pitches & 60 chalets**
Via Flaminia Nuova 821, 5mi/8km from the center. From Termini Station, take bus 910 to Piazza Mancini and then take bus 200. ✆ 06 33 32 604. www.campingflaminio.com. Closed Jan and Feb. ⌇

Shaded by acacia trees, this campsite has a restaurant, a grocery store, an open-air swimming pool, Internet access and a residential area for chalets. In high season, the staff organize activities like games and dance lessons.

Happy Camping

€　　**150 pitches & 500 bungalows**
Via Prato della Corte 1915, 6mi/10km from the center.
From Termini Station, take Metro line A to Piazzale Flaminio, then the train to Prima Porta and a shuttle bus that operates between 8.30am–noon and 5am–10.30pm. ✆ 06 33 62 64 01. www.happycamping.net. Open Mar–Oct. ⌇

This pleasant campsite in the northwest of the city has shaded, terraced clearings on which to pitch your tent, as well as electrical outlets for caravans, bathrooms with free showers, laundry facilities, and drinking-water fountains. There is also a restaurant, a bar, a supermarket, a children's playground and a good-sized swimming pool.

HOTELS

ROME

Certain entries (churches, galleries, bars, etc.) have been grouped together under **bold headings**. For complete lists of hotels, markets, restaurants, and shops, see the Must Do, Must Eat, and Must Stay sections in the guide.

156

INDEX

INDEX

List of Maps

Use the maps in this guide to explore the many different areas of the city.
All the maps are oriented north, unless otherwise indicated by a directional arrow.
To enable you to find your way around more easily, most place names are given
in Italian. Use Michelin's star ratings system to ensure that you don't miss the best
and most interesting sights, particularly if this is your first time in Rome or if you
are a little pressed for time.